Upgrade German Reading

Material written by: Alan Wesson
Commissioning Editor: Clive Bell
Content Editor: Naomi Laredo/Small Print
Series Designer: Michael Spencer
Designer: Naomi Laredo/Small Print
Cover Photo: C. Adam/Alamy
Cover Design: Kaya Cully
Illustrations by: Carl Flint (all cartoons) and Nigel Kitching (pages 8, 19, 22, 31, 40, 42, 43, 46, 47, 52, 64, 74)
Photo Credits: page 10: M. Gerber/Corbis; page 19: S.J. Laredo/Small Print; page 26: Mary Glasgow Magazines; page 41: K. Maack/Nordicphotos.com/Alamy; page 49: Bananastock; page 53: Hemera (top left), Bananastock; page 54: Hemera

Printed and bound in the UK by Ashford Colour Press Ltd, Gosport, Hampshire

Upgrade: German Reading

Contents

Upgrade: German Reading

Note to teachers

➤ **Upgrade: German Reading** is designed to enable all students to improve their reading skills and to achieve their highest possible examination grade. At Foundation, Foundation/Higher and Higher tiers, it provides clear analysis of and guidance through a wide range of texts, with tasks and tests that match closely the structure and content of those offered by the Awarding Bodies/Examination Boards. Solutions to all tasks and tests are provided on pages 76–79.

➤ The approach is both rigorous and humorous, with the intention of reassuring students that German, though sometimes challenging, can be enjoyable and, most importantly, manageable.

Features

➤ Covering most of the major themes and topics of the GCSE specifications, the book consists of 12 sections, most with two Foundation pages, a Foundation/Higher page and a Higher page. Some of the more demanding topics have just one Foundation page and two Foundation/Higher or Higher pages.

Tasks, learning skills and grammar

➤ At Foundation tier there are *Clever clues* which give students guidance on reading strategies, vocabulary patterns and basic grammar features.

➤ At Foundation/Higher tier *Handy hints* perform the same function, with a greater emphasis on grammatical features, whilst at Higher tier *Tips for texts* enable students to refine their higher-level reading skills and to deepen their understanding of grammar in general.

Vocabulary

➤ Every second section is followed by *Vital Vocabulary* sheets, which support students' understanding of the basic vocabulary and idioms of the topic sections. The Higher tier *Vital Vocabulary* sheets also provide specific support relating to the authentic texts on which students are tested. All of the *Vital Vocabulary* sheets suggest useful ways in which students could record and memorize vocabulary, idioms and structures.

Exam practice

➤ After every three sections there is an examination practice section, entitled **Test yourself**, covering a range of grades from Foundation tier to Higher tier.

➤ Solutions are provided on pages 76–79 to enable teachers or students to mark the **Test yourself** questions.

➤ Finally, there is a comprehensive glossary of rubrics on page 5, to ensure that students will be able to understand what is required of them whatever examination syllabus they follow, and the tables on pages 6–7 cross-reference the material in the book to all the major GCSE syllabuses/specifications.

B	Beantworte die Fragen (auf Deutsch).	Answer the questions (in German).
E	Ergänze die Sätze.	Complete the sentences.
F	Füll die Lücken (mit dem passenden Namen) aus.	Fll in the gaps (with the name that matches).
	Füll die Tabelle aus.	Fill in the grid.
L	Lies (jetzt) den Text über Irma/Elias.	(Now) read the text about Irma/Elias.
	Lies den Brief.	Read the letter.
	Lies den Text (noch einmal).	Read the text (again).
	Lies die Sätze (unten).	Read the sentences (below).
	Lies die Texte.	Read the texts.
	Lies die „Vox pops".	Read the 'vox pops'.
M	Mach zwei Listen auf Englisch.	Make two lists in English.
S	Schreib „Anja", „Melanie" oder „Judith" auf.	Write down 'Anja', 'Melanie' or 'Judith'.
	Schreib den Namen der richtigen Stadt auf.	Write down the name of the correct city.
	Schreib den passenden Namen auf.	Write down the name that matches.
	Schreib den richtigen Buchstaben in jedes Kästchen.	Write the correct letter in each box.
	Schreib die Distanzen auf.	Write down the distances.
	Schreib jeweils den richtigen Namen auf.	Write down the correct name each time.
	Schreib R (richtig), F (falsch) oder ? (nicht im Text).	Write R (true), F (false) or ? (not in the text).
	Schreib U, E, 1, 2 oder 3 in das Kästchen.	Write U, E, 1, 2 or 3 in the box.
W	Wähl den richtigen Buchstaben.	Choose the correct letter.
	Wähl die passenden Wörter.	Choose the words that match.
	Wähl die richtige Uhrzeit.	Choose the correct time.
	Wähl einen Job für jede Person.	Choose a job for each person.
	Wähl entweder A, B, C oder D.	Choose from A, B, C or D.
	Was ist das?	What is that?
	Was passt zusammen?	What goes together?
	Wer …?	Who …?
	Wer ist das?	Who is that?
	Wer meint das?	Whose opinion is that?

AQA Themes/Modules

Theme/Module 1: My World

1A Self, Family and Friends: pages 9, 10, 11, 68

1B Interests and Hobbies: pages 12, 13, 14, 15, 53

1C Home and Local Environment: pages 8, 18, 19, 20, 21

Theme/Module 2: Holiday Time and Travel

2A Travel, Transport and Finding the way: pages 24, 25, 26, 27

2B Tourism and 2C Accommodation: pages 30, 31, 32, 33, 35, 37

2D Holiday Activities and 2E Services: pages 34, 36

Theme/Module 3: Work and Lifestyle

3A Home Life: pages 42, 43

3B Healthy Living: pages 44, 45

3D Leisure: pages 48, 49, 52, 54, 55

3E Shopping: pages 46, 47

Theme/Module 4: The Young Person in Society

4A Character and Personal Relationships: pages 58, 59, 60, 61

4B The Environment and 4E Social Issues, Choices and Responsibilities: pages 64, 65, 66, 67, 70

4C Education and 4D Careers and Future Plans: pages 69, 71

Edexcel topic areas

At home and abroad
- Things to see and do: pages 12, 13, 18, 19, 20
- Weather and climate: page 35
- Travel, transport and directions: pages 24, 25, 26, 27
- Holidays, tourist information and accommodation: pages 30, 31, 32, 37
- Services and shopping abroad: pages 34, 36, 46, 47

Education, training and employment
- Different types of jobs: page 68
- Future plans and work experience: pages 48, 49, 69, 71

House, home and daily routine
- Types of home: pages 8, 21
- Information about self, family and friends: pages 9, 11, 58, 59, 60, 61
- Helping around the house: page 42
- Food and drink: pages 43, 44, 45

Media, entertainment and youth culture
- Sport, entertainment and fashion: pages 49, 54, 55
- Famous personalities: page 10
- Current affairs, social and environmental issues: pages 64, 65, 66, 67

Social activities, fitness and health
- Free time (evenings, weekends, meeting people): pages 48, 52, 53
- Special occasions: page 33
- Hobbies, interests, sports and exercise: pages 12, 13, 14, 15
- Shopping and money matters: pages 46, 47
- Accidents, injuries, common ailments and health issues (smoking, drugs): page 70

OCR contexts

1 Everyday activities
- a Home life: pages 8, 21
- c Eating and drinking: pages 34, 43
- d Health and fitness: pages 44, 45, 70

2 Personal and social life
- a People – the family and new contacts: pages 9, 11, 42, 58, 59, 60, 61, 68
- b Free time: pages 12, 13, 14, 15, 48, 49, 53, 54, 55
- c Making appointments: page 52
- d Special occasions: page 33

3 The world around us
- a The local and other areas: pages 18, 19, 20, 21

- b Shopping and public services: pages 36, 46, 47
- c The environment: pages 35, 64, 65, 66, 67
- d Going places: pages 24, 25, 26, 27

4 The world of work
- b Careers and life-long learning: pages 69, 71

5 The international world
- b World issues, events and people: page 10
- c Tourism and holidays: pages 32, 37
- d Tourist and holiday accommodation: pages 30, 31

WJEC topics

Topic A

b Home life and school
- (i) Home life: pages 21, 42

c Food, health and fitness
- (i) Food: pages 34, 43
- (ii) Health and fitness: pages 44, 45, 70

Topic B

a Self, family and personal relationships: pages 9, 10, 11, 58, 59, 60, 61, 68

b Free time and social activities: pages 12, 13, 14, 15, 46, 47, 48, 49, 52, 53, 54, 55

c Holidays and special occasions: pages 24, 25, 26, 27, 36

Topic C

a Home town and local area: page 20

b Natural and made environment: page 35

c People, places and customs: page 33

Topic D

b Careers and employment: pages 48, 49, 69, 71

Topic E

a Tourism at home and abroad: pages 18, 19, 30, 31, 32, 36, 37

b Life in other countries and communities: page 37

c World events and issues: pages 64, 65, 66, 67

CCEA topics

1 Everyday Activities
- (a) Home and school life: pages 21, 42
- (b) Food and drink: pages 43, 44, 45
- (c) Shopping: pages 46, 47
- (d) Eating out: page 34

2 Personal Life and Social Relationships
- (a) Self, family and friends: pages 9, 10, 11, 58, 59, 60, 61
- (b) Health: page 70
- (c) Leisure activities: pages 12, 13, 14, 15, 48, 49, 52, 53, 54, 55
- (d) Celebrations and special occasions: page 33

3 The World Around Us
- (a) House and home: page 8
- (b) Town and countryside: pages 18, 19, 20
- (c) Getting around: pages 24, 25, 26, 27
- (d) Weather: page 35

4 The World of Work
- (a) Services to the public: page 36
- (b) Occupations and places of work: page 68
- (c) Future plans and careers: pages 69, 71

5 The International World
- (a) Travel and tourism: pages 30, 31, 32
- (b) Life in countries or communities in which the target language is spoken: page 37
- (c) Caring for the environment: pages 64, 65, 66, 67

Standard Grade topics and topic development

Basic topics

- Name, age, domicile, nationality, cardinal points: pages 8, 10, 11, 20, 21

- Members of family, friends, physical and character description, problems and relationships: pages 9, 58, 59, 60, 61

- Routine: page 42

- Leisure, sports, healthy eating, drugs, TV, film: pages 12, 13, 14, 15, 44, 45, 48, 49, 52, 53, 54, 55, 70

- Foods/drinks: page 43

- Snack food, restaurants: page 34

- Simple directions: page 25

- Buildings, tourist information, helping the environment: pages 18, 19, 24, 37, 64, 65, 66, 67

- Simple transactions, jobs/work and study, work experience, future employment: pages 30, 31, 36, 46, 47, 68, 69, 71

- Travel information, travel plans: pages 24, 25, 26, 27, 33

- Weather, future and past holidays: pages 26, 27, 32, 35

1 Wo wohnst du? Schreib den richtigen Buchstaben in jedes Kästchen. (5 marks)

Beispiel:

Ich wohne in einer Wohnung in einer Großstadt. ☐ F

1 Ich wohne auf einem Bauernhof auf dem Land. ☐

2 Ich wohne in einem Reihenhaus in einer kleinen Stadt. ☐

3 Ich wohne in einem großen Haus in einem Dorf. ☐

4 Ich wohne in einem Doppelhaus am Rande der Stadt. ☐

5 Ich wohne in einem Bungalow mit einem kleinen Garten. ☐

That house doesn't look at all 'gross' to me. It looks quite nice!

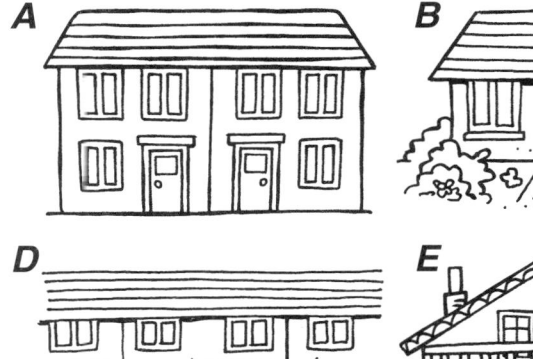

A   B   C

D   E   F

Mein Haus ist nicht sehr groß, aber sehr bequem!

➤ Look for familiar words like **ich wohne**. This tells you all the sentences must be about … what?

➤ Some set phrases are worth learning by heart. Can you work out what **auf dem Land** (sentence 1) means? It's a bit like the English.

➤ Some words for places to live (**Bungalow**, sentence 5!) are similar to the English. And a **Doppelhaus** (sentence 4) is a 'double house' – what do you think that means?

➤ If you're not sure of the words for what people live in, use a process of elimination! The ones with **-haus** in must be a kind of house, so **Bauernhof** (sentence 1) must be something else – and what other sort of building do you find in the **Land**?

If you're still stuck, check in the *Vital Vocabulary* (worksheet 16). Why not start a little notebook? If you note down the words you found hard, you'll find them easier to learn next time round.

Clever clues

Name/
Group:

▼ Who is your hero or role-model?
We asked some young people in Bonn …

A Sie heißt Anja. Sie ist Sängerin. Sie ist siebenundzwanzig und sie hat schwarze, lockige Haare und blaue Augen.

Johannes is 'achtundzwanzig'? Hey, he can't be 82!

B Er heißt Otto. Er ist Fußballspieler. Er ist einundzwanzig und er hat einen Bart und kurze, schwarze Haare. Er hat braune Augen.

C Sie heißt Monika. Sie ist Model. Sie ist neunzehn und sie hat schöne blonde Haare und grüne Augen.

Remember, German numbers from 20 to 99 are the other way round! So 'achtundzwanzig' is 28!

D Er heißt Johannes. Er ist Sänger. Er hat lange, braune Haare und er ist achtundzwanzig Jahre alt. Er hat einen braunen Schnurrbart und graue Augen.

1 Answer the questions. (5 marks)
Who …

Beispiel:
… has blue eyes and black curly hair?

Anja

1 … has a brown moustache and long brown hair?

_____

2 … is 19?

_____

3 … is 21 and has a beard?

_____

4 … has fair hair and green eyes?

_____

5 … is a singer and is 28?

_____

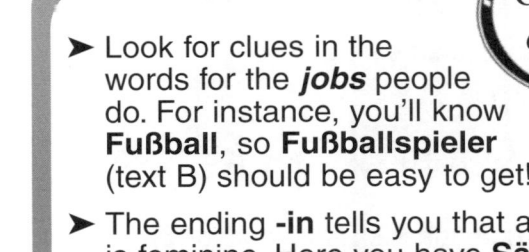

Clever clues

➤ Look for clues in the words for the *jobs* people do. For instance, you'll know **Fußball**, so **Fußballspieler** (text B) should be easy to get!

➤ The ending **-in** tells you that a word is feminine. Here you have **Sänger** and **Sängerin** (A & D), but look out for **-in** on other words too.

➤ **Bart** (B) has nothing to do with a well-known TV cartoon character! It's a 'hairy word'. And what about **Schnurrbart** (D)?

➤ Make sure you don't get the colours mixed up. **Blau** and **braun**, and **grau** and **grün**, are easy to confuse – but get them wrong and you could be talking blue or green hair!

Don't forget that the *Vital Vocabulary* (worksheet 16) can give you extra help if you need it.

☆ ☆ ☆ Eure Stars: Sarah Michelle Gellar

Sarah Michelle Gellar ist in Deutschland ein großer TV-Liebling. Alle mögen „Buffy – Im Bann der Dämonen", aber Sarah ist nicht nur als Fernseh-Star aktiv. Sie macht auch Kino-Filme und spielt Daphne in der Komödie „Scooby-Doo". Sie wurde 1977 in New York City geboren, aber sie wohnt jetzt in Kalifornien. Ihre Eltern sind geschieden und sie hat keine Geschwister, aber sie mag Haustiere gern und hat zwei Hunde, Thor und Tyson. Sie hat am 14. April Geburtstag und hat hellgrüne Augen und dunkelbraune Haare. Sie interessiert sich für Sport – besonders Fußball und Schlittschuhlaufen. Sie isst am liebsten Pasta und ihre Lieblingsfarbe ist rot.

1 Schreib **R** (richtig), **F** (falsch) oder **?** (nicht im Text). (6 marks)

Beispiel:
Sarah kommt aus New York. **R**

1 Sie hat zwei Brüder und eine Schwester. ☐

2 Sie hat keine Haustiere. ☐

3 Sarah hat blonde Haare. ☐

4 Sie interessiert sich für Fußball. ☐

5 Sie isst sehr gern Pommes frites. ☐

6 Ihre Lieblingsfarbe ist grün. ☐

2 Schreib den richtigen Buchstaben in jedes Kästchen. (5 marks)

Beispiel:
Sarah wohnt jetzt in **E**.

1 Ihre ☐ heißen Thor und Tyson.

2 Sarah ist am 14. ☐ geboren.

3 Sie hat ☐ Augen.

4 Sie isst gern ☐.

5 Sie mag die Farbe ☐ gern.

A	April
B	grüne
C	Pasta
D	Hunde
E	Kalifornien
F	Katzen
G	New York
H	rot

☞ Handy hints

➤ In German, the trick is to look for *parts* of words that give you a clue to the meaning of the whole word. So what does **Lieblings-** mean? Think of how you start a letter …

➤ 'C' by itself is usually a **K** in German – so if you read all 'k's as 'c's, words like **Komödie** and **aktiv** will be much easier to recognize.

➤ **Wurde … geboren** is a useful phrase. It usually comes up with a date and a place, so you should be able to get the meaning! And don't forget that the *auxiliary verb* **wurde** sends the participle **geboren** to the end of the clause or sentence.

➤ **Geschwister** is a tricky word – make sure you don't mix it up with **Schwester**.

➤ **Hell** hasn't got anything to do with the exam room! It comes up with colours and it's the opposite of **dunkel**. So has Sarah got light green hair, or what?

➤ Look for phrases in the questions that mean the same as something in the text, but use different words. **Wurde in … geboren** and **kommt aus …** (Ex 1, Beispiel) mean the same, or nearly the same, and so do **Lieblingsfarbe** and **mag die Farbe … gern** (Ex 2, Qu 5).

➤ Make sure you cross out the words as you fill them in from the list. That way, it will be easier to work out which are left.

Name/
Group:

Interview der Woche

Helena (15) aus Braunschweig möchte einmal Ballett-Tänzerin sein.

Ich wollte schon immer Ballett-Tänzerin werden. Mit drei Jahren habe ich einen Ballett-Rock bekommen und bin durch die Wohnung getanzt. Dann habe ich mir nur noch Ballett-Sachen gewünscht. Zu Weihnachten, zum Geburtstag wollte ich nur Ballett-Videos, Ballett-Bücher und Ballett-Klamotten haben. Ich habe mit fünf Jahren mit dem Ballett-Unterricht angefangen. Aber erst nachdem ich mit der Grundschule fertig war, also mit zehn Jahren, habe ich angefangen richtig zu trainieren. Jetzt habe ich jeden Nachmittag Ballett. Mein Ziel ist es jetzt, erst mal in eine Tanzklasse zu kommen. Ich möchte gern an der Hamburger Staatsoper oder in Wuppertal studieren. Ich trainiere im Moment für die Aufnahmeprüfungen. Ja, und wenn ich dann einmal Tänzerin bin, dann möchte ich natürlich auf allen großen Bühnen der Welt tanzen und als Primaballerina gefeiert werden.

Tips for texts

➤ In this text Helena is talking about what she *wanted* when she was younger. She uses the modal **wollte**, past tense of **wollen** – so you need to look at the *end* of the sentence for the main verb, which will give you the important information about what's going on.

➤ Don't confuse **mit drei Jahren** and **vor drei Jahren**. One is 'at the age of' – but what is the other?

➤ To say *not until*, German says 'first after' or 'first when'. Find the exact phrase and check what happens to the word order.

➤ Don't forget how German forms the *passive*. There's an example of it at the end of the text, with the word order reversed because it comes after **ich möchte**. And what else is the verb **werden** used for?

➤ In this text, there are lots of *word-order* issues to consider. See how many different reasons there are for the verb to go to the end or for the word order to be reversed.

➤ Keep an eye open for *tenses*. This text is in the past tense, and so are most of the questions in Ex 2 – so you will need to answer in the same way.

➤ If you need help with *tense forms*, use the ones in the questions and/or text as a model.

---

1 Make notes for a biography of Helena.

1 Describe what she did at the following ages. (3 marks)

   a Three: _____

   b Five: _____

   c Ten: _____

2 List three things she wanted and when she hoped to receive them. (3 marks)

   _____

   _____

   _____

3 List three ambitions she mentions. (3 marks)

   _____

   _____

   _____

2 Beantworte die Fragen auf Deutsch. (5 marks)

Beispiel:

Wie alt war Helena, als sie einen Ballett-Rock bekommen hat?   *Drei Jahre alt*

1 Was wollte sie zum Geburtstag oder zu Weihnachten bekommen?

   _____

2 Wie alt war sie, als sie ihre ersten Ballett-Stunden gehabt hat? _____

3 Wie alt war sie, als sie richtig zu trainieren angefangen hat? _____

4 Wie oft hat sie jetzt Ballett?

   _____

5 Wo möchte sie später studieren?

   _____

Name/
Group:

▼ You see this list of prices for activities on the wall at a German youth club.

Schwimmen	3 Euro
Reiten	4 Euro
Segeln	8 Euro
Kegeln	6 Euro
Tischtennis	2 Euro
Schlittschuhlaufen	5 Euro

I thought you said 'segeln', not 'kegeln'!

Clever clues

➤ Look for parts of words that you already know, like **-tennis**. Even if this doesn't give you the whole answer, it often gives you all you need to work it out.

➤ *Say* the words to yourself. **Reiten** may not *look* much like any of the answers, but it *sounds* like one …

➤ It's easy to get **segeln** and **kegeln** mixed up, because only one letter is different. However, this could help you as well – learn them as a pair. (**S**ailing and s**k**ittles could help you remember which is which!)

If you're still stuck, look up the words in the *Vital Vocabulary* (worksheet 16) – but make sure you don't forget them again! It's a good idea to keep a list of words you didn't know but have looked up.

1 You only have 5 euros. In the boxes, write the letters of the activities you can do for 5 euros each. (3 marks)

Beispiel:

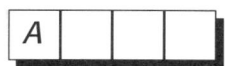

A			

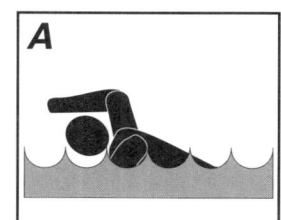

A

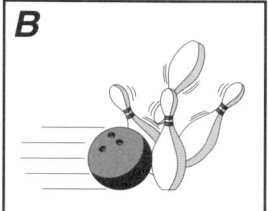

B

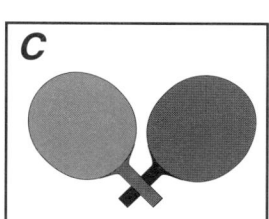

C

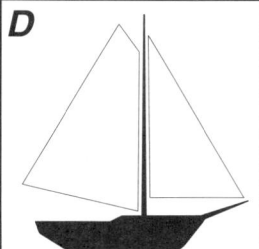

D

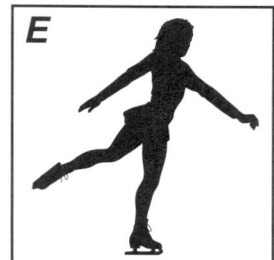

E

F

Name/
Group:

I turned up for the table tennis at ten past four. So where is everybody?!

'Vierzehn Uhr' is 14 hours! It's in the 24-hour clock!

1 Wähl die richtige Uhrzeit. (4 marks)

Austauschprogramm
für die britische Schülergruppe

Beispiel:

- Neun Uhr: Ankunft der britischen Austauschpartner   G
- Mittag: Ankunftsparty in der Aula   ☐
- Vierzehn Uhr: Tischtennis für alle!   ☐
- Schwimmparty am Freibad! Pünktlich um sechzehn Uhr   ☐
- Ab 20 Uhr: Disko. Bring einen Freund/eine Freundin mit!   ☐

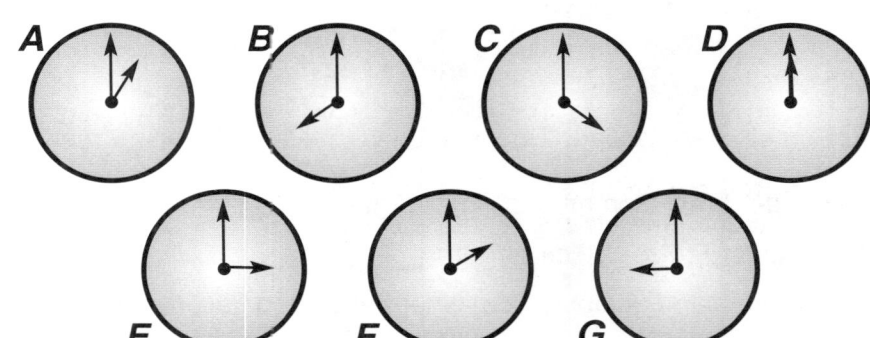

☞ Handy hints

➤ There's an easy way to convert times in the 24-hour clock to 'ordinary' 12-hour times: just take 12 off the number given. So **20 Uhr** becomes 8 o'clock and **19 Uhr** becomes …?

➤ Don't be confused by words that you don't need to know. You may not know **Austausch**, for instance – but it doesn't actually matter here!

➤ Look out for words you may know from **other contexts**. For example, you could have met **Ankunft** and **kommt … an** when asking about trains.

➤ Use **common sense**! For instance, you shouldn't need to be a fluent German speaker to work out what **Schwimmparty** means.

➤ If you see prepositions 'hanging around' in odd places, check if they are part of a **separable verb** that you hadn't noticed! Which verb is **bring … mit** from?

If you need to, look at the *Vital Vocabulary* (worksheet 16) – but make sure you don't learn the same words over and over again! Cross out the ones you've already learnt, or keep a little notebook with a list in English and German of the words you find hardest to remember.

Name/
Group:

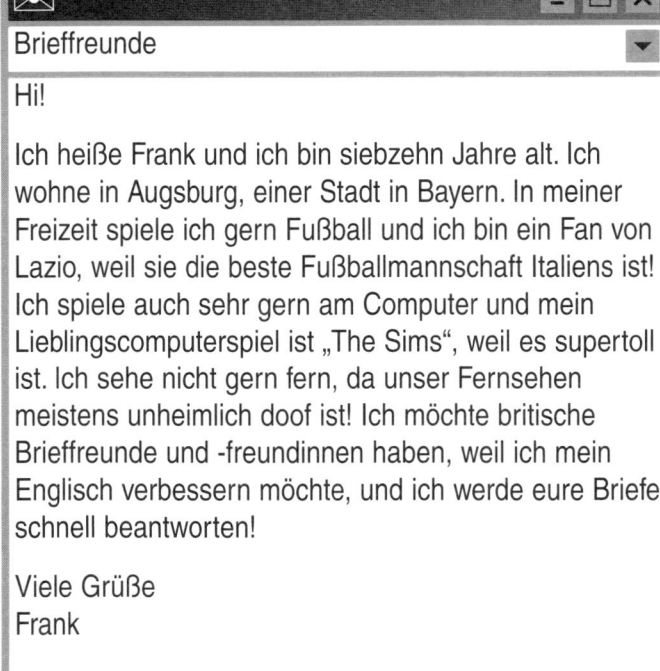

7 Schreib den richtigen Buchstaben in jedes Kästchen. (5 marks)

Beispiel: Frank kommt aus Augsburg, einer C in Bayern.

1 In seiner Freizeit spielt er gern ☐.

2 Frank ist ein Fan von Lazio, einer bekannten italienischen ☐.

3 Am liebsten spielt Frank ein ☐, das „The Sims" heißt.

4 Er findet deutsches ☐ ganz doof.

5 Er sucht einen britischen ☐ oder eine britische Brieffreundin.

A Name
B Fußball
C Stadt
D Deutschland
E Fußballmannschaft
F Brieffreund
G Fernsehen
H Computerspiel
I Jahre

☞ Handy hints

➤ Don't panic if you don't understand all the words in the list! There are usually more than you need, and sometimes the ones you don't understand are the ones you don't need.

➤ Be systematic! Don't try to fill in the words in the order of the blanks, but read the text through several times first. Then fill the blanks you are sure about first.

➤ Make sure you cross out the words as you fill them in from the list. That way, it will be easier to work out which are left.

➤ Look for clues about a particular blank which come earlier or later in the text. For instance, in one sentence you have **Ich spiele auch sehr gern am …**, and later you have **mein Lieblingscomputerspiel ist …**: what clues does the second phrase give you about what goes in Qu 1?

Name/
Group:

1 — Freizeitstress —

In Deutschland hat jeder Zwölfte Freizeit-stress. Freizeitstress ist zum Beispiel, wenn man zu viel Programm hat, wenn man keine Ideen hat, wenn es keine Freizeitangebote gibt oder wenn Freizeit wie harte Arbeit ist. Besonders schlimm ist Freizeitstress bei Leuten zwischen vierzehn und neunundzwanzig Jahren. Und doppelt so viele Leute auf dem Land haben Freizeitstress wie Leute in den Großstädten. Freizeitstress kann vieles sein. Kennst du ihn?

1 Lies die Sätze. Schreib **R** (richtig), **F** (falsch) oder **?** (nicht im Text). (4 marks)

Beispiel:
Freizeitstress kann ein Problem für Jugendliche sein. ☐ R

1 Freizeitstress kann man haben, wenn man zu viel machen möchte. ☐

2 Man kann auch an Freizeitstress leiden, wenn man nicht weiß, was man machen soll. ☐

3 Freizeitstress ist ein sehr großes Problem für ältere Leute. ☐

4 Die meisten Leute, die Freizeitstress haben, wohnen in großen Städten. ☐

Tips for texts

➤ Make sure you understand key words before trying to do the exercises. **Freizeitstress** occurs a lot here, and half of the word is easy – but make sure you understand the other half as well!

➤ Look out for different ways of saying the same thing. Exam questions often *paraphrase* the text – in other words, they say the same thing in a different way. For example, **man hat zu viel Programm** and **man möchte zu viel machen** (Qu 1) mean roughly the same.

➤ Use grammar clues:

• Look for words like **weil** and **wenn**, and don't forget what these do to word order.

• Don't miss modal verbs like **kann**: these also affect word order, and they *always* have another verb with them, which is actually the important one. Find that first!

'Freizeitstress'? Nah!

2 Skateboards

Sie kommen aus Amerika. In den 60er Jahren fuhren die Surfboarder mit ihnen am kalifornischen Strand entlang, wenn das Meer zu ruhig zum Surfen war. Damals waren sie aus Holz. In den 70er Jahren bekamen sie bessere Räder und Skateboarden wurde zu einer Modewelle. Auch die Bretter wurden immer besser. Heute sind sie aus Aluminium, Plastik und Fiberglas. Besonders bei den Kids in den Großstädten sind Skateboards im Moment total beliebt. Sie sind eine gute Alternative zum Inlineskaten und zum Kickboardfahren.

2 Beantworte die Fragen.

Beispiel: Woher kommen Skateboards?

  Aus den USA

1 Wann fuhren die Surfboarder der 60er Jahre Skateboard?

_____ (1 mark)

2 Welchen Vorteil hatten die Skateboards der 70er Jahre?

_____ (1 mark)

3 Aus welchen Materialien sind die Skateboards von heute? _____

_____ (3 marks)

4 Wer geht am liebsten skateboarden?

_____ (1 mark)

Name/
Group:

Vital Vocabulary

I learn my words by putting my biscuits in a row. The more words I learn, the more biscuits I get to eat! It works for people too …

Personal details

◆ Foundation and ◆ ◆ Foundation/Higher (WS 8–10)

Nouns

Masculine

der Bart	*beard*
der Bauernhof	*farm*
der Fernseh-Star	*TV star*
der Fußball(spieler)	*football (player)*
der Garten	*garden*
der Geburtstag	*birthday*
der Kino-Film	*cinema film*
der Liebling	*favourite, darling*
der Schnurrbart	*moustache*
der/die Sänger(in)	*singer*

Feminine

die Komödie	*comedy*
die Stadt	*town*

Neuter

das (Doppel)haus	*(semi-detached) house*
das Dorf	*village*
das Haustier	*pet*
das Reihenhaus	*terraced house*
das Schlittschuhlaufen	*ice-skating*

Plural

die Augen	*eyes*
die Geschwister	*brothers and sisters, siblings*
die Haare	*hair*

Verbs and useful expressions

blau	*blue*
blond	*blond, fair*
braun	*brown*
dunkel	*dark*
essen	*to eat*
geboren	*born*
geschieden	*divorced*
grau	*grey*
groß	*big*
grün	*green*
heißen	*to be called*
hell	*pale, light*
sich interessieren für	*to be interested in*
klein	*small*
kurz	*short*
auf dem Land	*in the country*
lang	*long*
Lieblings-	*favourite …*
am liebsten	*best of all*
lockig	*curly*
mögen	*to like*
am Rande der Stadt	*on the edge of town*
rot	*red*
schön	*beautiful*
schwarz	*black*
spielen	*to play*
wohnen	*to live*

Interests and hobbies

◆ Foundation and ◆ ◆ Foundation/Higher (WS 12–14)

Nouns

Masculine

der Austausch	*exchange*
der Brieffreund/ die Brieffreundin	*penfriend*

Feminine

die Ankunft	*arrival*
die Aula	*hall*
die Freizeit	*free time*
die (Fußball)mannschaft	*(football) team*
die Großstadt	*large town, city*

Neuter

das Computerspiel	*computer game*
das Fernsehen	*television*
das Freibad	*open-air pool*
das Programm	*programme, schedule*
das Tischtennis	*table tennis*

Verbs and useful expressions

beantworten	*to answer*
doof	*stupid*
fernsehen	*to watch TV*
kegeln	*to play skittles*
mitbringen	*to bring (with one)*
pünktlich	*punctual(ly), on time*
reiten	*to ride*
schwimmen	*to swim*
segeln	*to sail*
verbessern	*to improve, correct*

It's easier to learn words in stages: try learning the masculine words first, then the feminine, and so on.

Name/
Group:

Vital Vocabulary

Try writing the English words on one side of a pack of blank cards and the German on the other. Carry the cards around, and every now and then shuffle them and test yourself on a word – or be mean and test your friends!

Personal details
◆ ◆ ◆ Higher (WS 11)

Nouns	
Masculine	
der Ballett-Rock	ballet skirt, tutu
der (Ballett-)Unterricht	(ballet) lessons, instruction
Feminine	
die (Aufnahme)prüfung	(entrance) exam
die Bühne	stage
die Grundschule	primary school
die (Staats)oper	(state) opera
die Tänzerin	dancer
die (Tanz)klasse	(dance) class, school
die Welt	world
die Wohnung	flat, apartment
Neuter	
das Ziel	aim, goal
Plural	
die Klamotten	gear, clothes
die Sachen	things, stuff

Verbs and useful expressions	
anfangen	to begin
bekommen	to get
durch	through
erst nachdem	only after, not until
feiern	to celebrate, fête
fertig	ready, finished, 'through'
zum Geburtstag	for (my) birthday
jeden Nachmittag	every afternoon
mit drei Jahren	when (I was) three
studieren	to study
trainieren	to train, practise
zu Weihnachten	for Christmas
werden	to become, be
wollen	to want
sich (dat.) wünschen	to wish (for oneself)

Interests and hobbies
◆ ◆ ◆ Higher (WS 15)

Nouns	
Masculine	
der Freizeitstress	free-time stress, leisure-time stress
der Strand	beach
Feminine	
die Arbeit	work
die Idee	idea
die Modewelle	fashion, craze
Neuter	
das Brett	board
das Freizeitangebot	leisure opportunities
das Meer	sea
das Rad (Räder)	wheel(s)
Plural	
die Leute	people

Verbs and useful expressions	
(total) beliebt	(extremely) popular
damals	at that time
doppelt so viele	twice as many
entlangfahren	to go along
hart	hard
aus Holz	made of wood
jeder Zwölfte	every twelfth (person), one (person) in twelve
kalifornisch	Californian
auf dem Land	in the country
leiden	to suffer
zu viel Programm haben	to have too much on
ruhig	calm
schlimm	bad
zwischen	between

A good way to learn words is to look at the German but say the English (without peeping!). Then do it the other way round, which is harder!

Name/ Group:

i

Schloss: montags geschlossen
Dom: sonntags geschlossen
Museum: nur an Wochenenden geöffnet
Zoo: donnerstags und freitags
geschlossen

Remember, 'geschlossen' has nothing to do with having had too many beers!

1 In the boxes, write the letters of the things you can visit on each of the following days.

Beispiel: on Sundays: | A | B | C |

1 on Mondays:
(2 marks)

2 on Fridays:
(2 marks)

3 on Wednesdays:
(3 marks)

A    *B*    *C*    *D*

Clever clues

➤ Don't be put off by pairs of words like **geschlossen** and **geöffnet**: if you know one, you can work out the other. And if you take off **ge-** (which is the beginning of most past participles), the word that means 'open' begins with **ö** and the one that means 'shut' begins with **s**!

➤ More importantly, you know from the *questions* that this is a text telling you when things are open and closed, so that's another clue to the meanings of those words.

➤ Make sure you remember words like the days of the week, months, etc. – it would be silly to lose marks for not knowing these! Check that you know **Dienstag**, **Mittwoch** and **Donnerstag** in particular, as these aren't like the English. People often mix up **Dienstag** and **Donnerstag**, so learn them carefully.

➤ Take care to use any clues in the pictures. You may not know what **Dom** means, but if you know **Schloss**, **Zoo** and **Museum**, you can work out from the pictures what the other place must be!

Don't forget that the *Vital Vocabulary* (worksheet 28) can help you, but learn groups of words like the days and months as a block (all 7 days and 12 months), so that you can run through them quickly in your head when you need them.

Name/
Group:

DOM

So it doesn't have to have a dome to be called that!

➤ Make sure you understand the question in the instruction. This one looks hard, but it's a common way of asking questions that exam boards often use.

➤ In fact, what it's asking is pretty much common sense, although you need to check for negatives, because you might be being asked what *isn't* in a particular town!

➤ Look out for familiar words in different forms. You may not recognize **Läden** (3rd bullet), but it's the plural of **Laden**, which you probably know. Familiar words often have odd-looking plurals!

➤ Don't be put off by words you don't need to know. You may not know **Fachwerkhäuser(n)** (5th bullet), but it's quite likely that you do know **Marktplatz**, which appears with it.

Check any remaining words in the *Vital Vocabulary* (worksheet 28) – but don't waste time looking up *compound words* when you've already met the words they're made up of. Look out for these and use them to help you: for instance, you shouldn't have to look up **Altstadt**, because you should know **alt** and **Stadt**.

---

1 Was gibt es in Marburg zu sehen und zu tun? Schreib den richtigen Buchstaben in jedes Kästchen. (5 marks)

Marburg ...

Ferienort für die ganze Familie!

✿ **Altstadt mit Schloss**

✿ **interessante Museen**

✿ **Läden für alle**

✿ **wunderschöne Landschaft**

✿ **Marktplatz mit Fachwerkhäusern**

✿ **historischer Dom**

Beispiel:

D

Ich **wohne** in einer Kleinstadt in Bayern. Die Stadt gefällt mir gar nicht. Die Landschaft ist uninteressant, die Stadtmitte ist hässlich und es gibt gar nichts für Jugendliche – nicht einmal eine Schule! Es gibt nur ein paar Häuser, eine Kirche, ein höchst langweiliges Museum – und einen Bahnhof, so dass man wegfahren kann. Hurra!

Anita, **16**, Drosselmühle, Bayern

'Ein paar Häuser'?! It must be a really small town if there's only a pair of houses!

It's not as small as all that! 'Ein Paar' is a pair, but 'ein paar' is a few.

Ich **wohne** in einer Großstadt in Norddeutschland. Die Stadtmitte ist ziemlich schön und es gibt sehr viel für Jugendliche – ein Sportzentrum, viele Geschäfte, ein Stadion und einen schönen Park, wo man im Sommer Fußball spielen kann. Es gibt einen Bahnhof, einen Flughafen und einen Busbahnhof, und meine Schule ist fast neu.

Christina, **17**, Geestheim, Schleswig-Holstein

1 Schreib **R** (richtig), **F** (falsch) oder **?** (nicht im Text). (5 marks)

Beispiel: In Drosselmühle gibt es eine Kirche. $\boxed{R}$

1 In Geestheim gibt es gar nichts für Jugendliche. ☐

2 In Drosselmühle kann man Fußball spielen. ☐

3 In Drosselmühle gibt es eine neue Schule. ☐

4 In Geestheim gibt es viele Sportmöglichkeiten. ☐

5 In Drosselmühle gibt es keinen Bahnhof. ☐

☞ Handy hints

➤ Make sure you understand *negatives*. One of these texts is negative and the other positive, so negative words like **kein**, **nicht**, **nichts**, **uninteressant**, **hässlich** and perhaps even **nur** are very important.

➤ If you have two texts where one is positive and one negative, as here, look for clues in one text that might help you with the other. One is often saying roughly the opposite of the other!

➤ Don't forget set phrases like **es gibt** and **man kann** – they are very often used in descriptions, and they are also useful in your oral and written exams for talking about where you live.

Check any remaining words in the *Vital Vocabulary* (worksheet 28), and try to learn all the 'town and local area' vocabulary together, because there's a lot of it and it's important.

Name/
Group:

Das Leben in der Stadtmitte

Ich wohne in einem Neubau in der Stadtmitte. In dieser Gegend sind die Gebäude meistens fünf Stockwerke hoch. Es ist ziemlich ruhig. Die Leute sind freundlich und es gibt hier Ordnung. Ich wohne gern hier.

Zwischen den Gebäuden gibt es viele Rasen mit Bäumen und Blumenbeeten. Auf einigen Balkons hängen Wäscheleinen und draußen gibt es normalerweise Spielzeug und Kleinkinder.

Die Bushaltestelle ist nicht weit von der Wohnung, und mit dem Bus kann ich in zehn Minuten das Einkaufszentrum erreichen. Aber meistens ist das nicht nötig, da wir hier eine Klinik, eine Apotheke, eine Grundschule und eine Post haben.

Wir haben eine kleine Dreizimmerwohnung mit Balkon. Die Wohnung ist im vierten Stock. Es gibt einen Aufzug, aber die meisten Familienmitglieder benutzen normalerweise die Treppe, weil der Aufzug oft außer Betrieb ist. Für meine Großmutter ist das ein großes Problem, weil sie die Treppe nicht gut hinaufsteigen kann.

Möchte ich ein Haus am Rande der Stadt haben? Vielleicht, aber ich bin völlig zufrieden mit meinem Leben hier in der Stadtmitte. Eines Tages werde ich ein Haus mit einem Garten kaufen, damit ich dort eine Katze haben kann. Im Moment ist das aber nur ein Traum, weil ich noch lange sparen muss …

Dietmar Vögele, 19, Dresden

Tips for texts

➤ As usual, break up words. You may not know **Neubau**, but what do **neu** and **Bau** mean?

➤ **Stockwerke** is a plural form of a word you probably know, used for talking about buildings – but which one?

➤ **Wir haben**, **Es ist/es sind** and **Es gibt** can all introduce sentences saying what there is or what someone has. However, only *one* of them is followed by the **nominative**. Which one?

➤ Look for **prepositions** which can give you information about what is where – and make a note of which ones are followed by the **dative** and which by the **accusative**.

➤ If you don't know a word, look at the context. If you're puzzled by **Aufzug**, finding out that another way to get to the flat is via the **Treppe** may help you to work it out. And that could help you with **außer Betrieb** as well!

➤ Look at the **questions** for different ways of phrasing sentences in the text that you don't understand. If you find **mit dem Bus kann ich … das Einkaufszentrum erreichen** difficult, the question **Wie lange dauert die Busreise ins Einkaufszentrum?** (Qu 3) may give you a clue.

➤ In your answers, you'll need to use several words for giving **reasons**, such as **damit** and **weil**. Don't forget what these do to the word order of your answer!

Finally, if you need vocabulary help, don't forget the *Vital Vocabulary* (worksheet 29).

---

1 Beantworte die Fragen auf Deutsch. (7 marks)

Beispiel:
Wo wohnt Dietmar? *In einem Neubau in der Stadtmitte*

1 Wie ist seine Gegend? _____

2 Was gibt es zwischen den Gebäuden? _____

3 Wie lange dauert die Busreise ins Einkaufszentrum? _____

4 Warum fährt Dietmar nur selten dorthin? _____

5 In welchem Stock befindet sich seine Wohnung? _____

6 Warum benutzen die meisten Familienmitglieder die Treppe? _____

7 Warum möchte Dietmar ein Haus mit einem Garten? _____

Name/
Group:

Section A
Questions and answers in English

▼ Read these signs in a German town and answer the questions in English.

Rauchen verboten!

Rasen nicht betreten!

Altstadt 300 m (nur für Fußgänger)

1 What TWO things are you not allowed to do? (2 marks)

_____

_____

2 What is 300 metres away, and who is it for? (2 marks)

_____

_____

Section B
Fragen und Antworten auf Deutsch

▼ Schreib den richtigen Buchstaben in jedes Kästchen. (5 marks)

Umfrage: „Wie ist deine Tagesroutine?"

Ich stehe um halb sieben auf.

1 Ich wasche mich um Viertel vor acht.

2 Ich gehe um acht Uhr zur Schule.

3 Ich komme um halb zwei nach Hause.

4 Von vier bis sechs Uhr mache ich meine Hausaufgaben.

5 Um sieben Uhr essen wir Abendbrot.

Beispiel:

F

☐
☐
☐
☐
☐

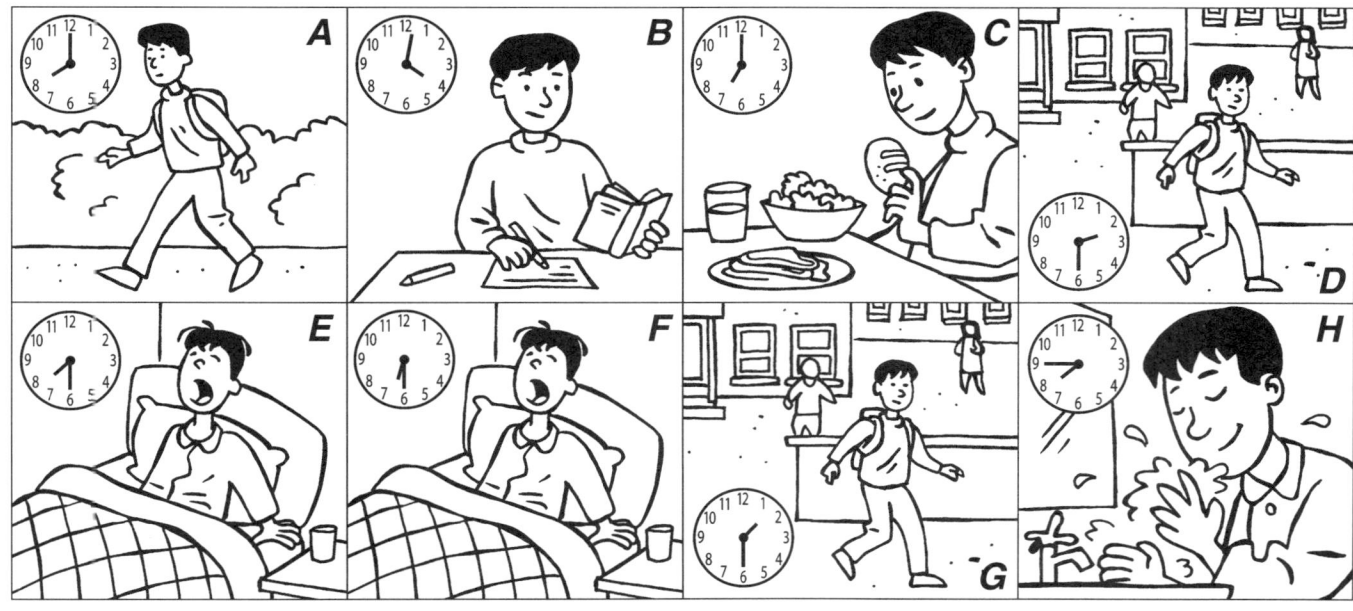

Name/
Group:

1

Musik, Musik

Wir haben mit Franziska (14) aus Hamburg über Musik gesprochen.

Frage: Franziska, was für Musik hörst du?
Franziska: Ach, ich höre eigentlich alles, was gerade im Radio gespielt wird oder auf MTV läuft.

Frage: Welche Musik findest du besonders gut?
Franziska: Ich mag am liebsten Popmusik, also Musik von Britney Spears, Nelly Furtado, Wheatus und so weiter. Aber ich bin kein Fan, also ich kaufe mir keine CDs von diesen Stars oder Bands. Ich höre diese Musik, so lange sie in der Hitparade ist. Wenn etwas Neues kommt, höre ich das.

Frage: Was für CDs kaufst du dir denn?
Franziska: Ich kaufe mir so CDs, wo Tracks von mehreren Leuten drauf sind, wie „Sommer-Hits 2003" oder so.

Frage: Ist Musik wichtig für dich?
Franziska: Ja, ich könnte ohne Musik nicht leben. Manche Tracks gehören einfach zu meinem Leben dazu. Madonnas „Don't Tell Me" zum Beispiel haben wir zu Weihnachten vor einem Jahr immer gehört. Ich hatte damals eine großartige Zeit. Und das Lied bringt mich immer noch in gute Stimmung, auch heute noch.

1 Lies den Text 1. Schreib **R** (richtig), **F** (falsch) oder **?** (nicht im Text). (5 marks)

Beispiel:
Franziska hört nicht gern Musik. [F]

1 Sie hört gern alles, was im Radio gespielt wird. ☐

2 Sie kauft nur Musik, die in der Hitparade ist. ☐

3 Sie kauft sich keine CDs von Britney Spears. ☐

4 Sie hört sehr gern Techno-Musik. ☐

5 Musik ist gar nicht wichtig für sie. ☐

2 Lies den Text 2 und die Sätze unten. Schreib den passenden Namen auf. Wer … (5 marks)

Beispiel: … würde Sport nur aufgeben, wenn er/sie krank wäre? _Anke_

1 … hat keine Idee, wie ein Leben ohne Sport wäre? _____

2 … kann Sport nicht leiden? _____

3 … hat viele Freunde, die auch gern Sport treiben? _____

4 … sieht fit aus, ist aber eigentlich gar nicht fit? _____

5 … würde Sport nur treiben, wenn es für seine Gesundheit nötig wäre? _____

2

Ist Sport wichtig für dich?

Sport macht Spaß, hält fit und bringt außerdem noch gute Laune, sagen die einen. Sport ist langweilig, anstrengend und macht auf Dauer nur den Körper kaputt, behaupten die anderen. Um herauszufinden, wie drei junge Dresdner über das Thema denken, haben wir Anke (17), Zoltan (18) und Johannes (16) gefragt, wie wichtig der Sport in ihrem Leben ist.

Unsere Frage: Wie wichtig ist Sport in eurem Leben?

Anke: Für mich ist Sport sehr wichtig. Ich würde nur auf Sport verzichten, wenn ich zum Beispiel krank wäre und keinen Sport machen könnte.

Johannes: *Für mich ist Sport auch unheimlich wichtig. Denn ohne Sport kann ich mir mein Leben wirklich nicht vorstellen. Meinen besten Freund habe ich beim Sport kennen gelernt, und auch was meine Freizeit angeht, ist Sport das, was achtzig Prozent meiner Zeit ausfüllt.*

Zoltan: Oh je, ich traue mich das ja schon fast nicht zu sagen, aber mir ist Sport völlig unwichtig, auch wenn das heute nicht besonders „in" ist. Zum Glück sieht man bei mir aber nicht, dass ich keinen Sport mache. Ich sehe eigentlich relativ fit aus. Ich glaube, wenn ich plötzlich total dick werden würde, würde ich vielleicht mit dem Sport anfangen. Aber nur vielleicht!

1 You're in a German station and you see the signs below.
Answer the questions.

NOTAUSGANG

If that's 'Not'
the 'Ausgang',
then what is it?

1 When would you use this door? (1 mark)

_____

Imbissstube neben dem
Fahrkartenschalter

2 Where is the snack bar? (1 mark)

_____

Gleis 1-3	Nahverkehr
Gleis 4-7	D-Züge
Gleis 8-10	InterCity-Züge und internationale Züge

3 What kinds of trains would you catch from these platforms? (3 marks)

1–3: _____

4–7: _____

8–10: _____

Clever clues

➤ What does the ***instruction*** tell you about where these notices are? This narrows it down for you: for example, there probably won't be a sign to a swimming pool!

➤ See if the ***questions*** provide any clues.

➤ Words ending in **-gang** are to do with 'going' (from **gehen**, 'to go'). Do you know **Eingang** and **Ausgang**, which are often seen on doors? (They are opposites.) To work out **Notausgang** (Qu 1), think what other kind of door is clearly marked in a public place. But beware! **Not** is a 'false friend': it doesn't mean 'not' (that would be too easy!), so what does it mean?

➤ Break up long words into smaller parts. You may not know **Stube** (Qu 2), but it's quite likely that you know **Imbiss**, which is the key part.

➤ You can probably recognize **internationale** (Qu 3) and you know that the notice is about types of train, so you should be able to work out what at least some of the others are.

If you still don't understand some of the notices, the *Vital Vocabulary* (worksheet 28) will help you learn the key words and others like them.

Name/
Group:

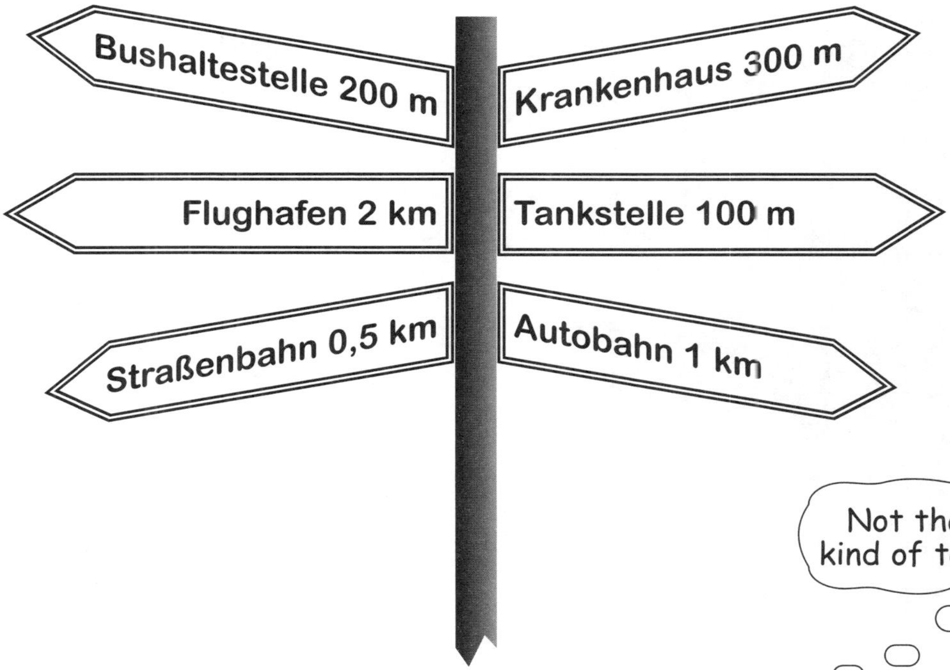

Bushaltestelle 200 m

Krankenhaus 300 m

Flughafen 2 km

Tankstelle 100 m

Straßenbahn 0,5 km

Autobahn 1 km

'Tankstelle'? I can't see any tanks – just cars and lorries!

Not that kind of tank!

1 In der Stadt: Wie weit ist das?
Schreib die Distanzen auf. (5 marks)

A

Beispiel:

_300 m_

B

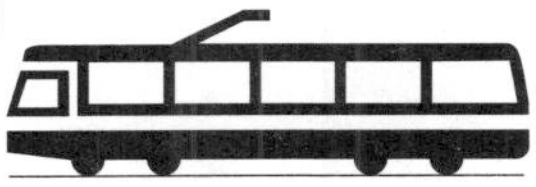

_____

C

_____

D

_____

E

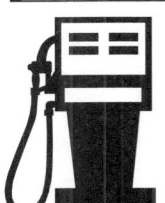

_____

F

_____

Clever clues

➤ Break the words up – that's nearly always worth doing with German words. They're like building blocks! **Flug** means 'flight'. Now can you work out **Flughafen**? And **Flugzeug**? And **Flugzeit**, **Flugstunde(n)** or **Flugkapitän**?

➤ Don't worry if there are parts of words (like **Haltestelle**) that you don't know. There's a good chance that you'll know the other part (**Bus**!).

➤ If that doesn't work, try lateral thinking! Sometimes German says things in a different way, but still a logical one. For instance, **Tankstelle** means 'tank place'. Now what could that be?

If you're still stuck, have a look at the _Vital Vocabulary_ (worksheet 28) – but don't forget to learn the words by heart before the exam!

Lieber Rudi,

morgen kommst du zu mir. Du fährst mit dem Zug von Halle nach Berlin und dein Zug kommt um Mittag hier in Berlin an. Ich warte auf dich vor dem Bahnhof. Die Fahrkarte kostet vierundzwanzig Euro hin und zurück (zweite Klasse, natürlich!) und dein Zug fährt um halb elf ab. Bring dein Geld mit und komm pünktlich am Bahnhof an. Und Achtung! Vergiss diesmal nicht – du kommst mit dem Zug und NICHT mit dem Bus!

Bis dann

Oma

1 Rudis Großmutter hat ihm diesen Brief geschrieben. Lies den Brief und ergänze die Sätze. (6 marks)

1 Rudi wohnt in _____.

2 Seine Großmutter trifft ihn vor dem _____.

3 Rudis Zug wird um _____ in Berlin sein.

4 Eine Rückfahrkarte kostet _____.

5 Rudi muss sein _____ mitbringen.

6 Rudi muss mit dem Zug kommen – er fährt nicht mit dem _____.

☞ Handy hints

➤ Think about who is writing (Rudi's grandma), and to whom (Rudi). Exam questions often concentrate on information about people, so this will give you lots of clues.

➤ German sentences are in the order **when** (time), **how** (manner), **where (to)** (place). If one of these three things is missing, the other two are still in this order.

➤ Don't forget that German **numbers** are 'backwards', so that 24 is 'four and twenty' – numbers in exams are often tricky ones!

➤ If two times are given, the earlier one will probably be when a train leaves and the later one when it arrives. But they don't always appear in that order! Don't get caught out – and make sure you learn **abfahren (fährt ... ab)** and **ankommen (kommt ... an)** for 'depart' and 'arrive'.

➤ Don't forget the 'examiner's favourite'! **Halb** means 'half to' and not 'half past' – so is **halb elf** half past ten or half past eleven?

➤ Use **common sense**! For instance, not many young people travel first class on the train ...

➤ Negatives (**nicht**, **kein**, etc.) are important! What's the difference between **er ist hier** and **er ist nicht hier**?

➤ Look out for **separable verbs**, where part of the verb separates and goes to the end of the sentence (e.g. **bring ... mit**, from **mitbringen**). The part that separates can be the key to the meaning.

Name/
Group:

1 Jasmin

Ich glaube, in der Zukunft wird man keinen Urlaub mehr machen, weil man virtuell verreisen wird. Ich glaube, es wird Zentren geben, wo man hingeht, wenn man Urlaub hat. Das sind Hotels, wo man isst, trinkt und schläft, die aber ganz in der Nähe des Hauses sind. Deshalb fährt man nicht mit dem Zug oder mit dem Auto und man fliegt auch nicht dorthin, sondern man kommt zu Fuß an und macht dann Cyber-Reisen. An einem Tag kann man die Pyramiden in Ägypten besuchen und am nächsten Tag den Grand Canyon. Die Fahrkarten sind kostenlos und es belastet die Umwelt nicht, weil man nicht wirklich dorthin fährt!

VIRTUELL SPAZIEREN!!

1 Füll die Lücken aus. (4 marks)

Beispiel:

Jasmin glaubt, in der Zukunft wird man nicht wirklich _verreisen_ .

1 Sie glaubt, es wird Zentren geben, wo man _____ machen wird.

2 In den Urlaubszentren wird man _____ machen können.

3 Die Fahrkarten werden _____ kosten.

4 Die Fahrten werden der _____ nicht schaden.

2 Wähl entweder A, B, C oder D. (4 marks)

Beispiel:

Nikolas glaubt, dass man künftig die Ferien
A in Spanien **B** zu Hause **C** in Russland
D im Weltraum
verbringen wird. [D]

1 Die Reise ins Weltraum-Hotel wird man mit
A einem Schiff **B** einem Auto **C** einem Raumschiff **D** einem Zug
machen. ☐

2 Die Reisen werden **A** sehr lang **B** sehr langweilig **C** sehr kurz **D** sehr teuer sein. ☐

3 Es wird **A** viele **B** keine **C** wenige **D** ein paar
Umweltprobleme geben. ☐

4 Man wird kurze Reisen mit dem
A Raum-Fahrrad **B** Raum-Zug **C** Raum-Auto **D** Raum-Bus
machen können. ☐

2 Nikolas

Ich glaube, in der Zukunft wird man im Weltraum Urlaub machen. Man wird in einem Raumschiff zu einem Weltraum-Hotel fahren. Die Reise wird nur ein paar Minuten dauern, da die Raumschiffe so schnell fahren. Zum Beispiel wird man um zehn Uhr morgens abfahren können und um Viertel nach zehn im Hotel ankommen. Die Fahrkarten werden sehr billig sein, weil die Technik alle Probleme gelöst haben wird und die Raumschiffe sehr wenig Kraftstoff verbrauchen werden. Umweltprobleme wird es auch nicht geben, weil wir anderswohin reisen werden! Dort wird man Tagesausflüge mit Raum-Fahrrädern machen können und künstliche Planeten besuchen können. Ja, im Weltraum-Hotel wird es wie im Paradies sein!

Tips for texts

➤ Don't be put off by long sentences in German! You can always break them down. It's much easier if you look for **clauses** between commas and treat them separately.

➤ You need to know where to find the **main verb**, as this is often the key to the meaning. Try looking at the end of the sentence after modals, the future tense (**werden**), etc.

➤ Look for familiar words that can help you to understand the gist of a text.

➤ Use grammar clues:

• What **tense** is the passage in? This will give you a lot of information.

• Sometimes the present tense is used to express the future, as in 'we are going next week'. Why is part of Jasmin's text in another tense here?

• Look for **word-order** clues. What does a future tense verb do to the word order? What do words like **weil** and **wenn** do?

Name/
Group:

Home and local environment
◆ Foundation and ◆ ◆ Foundation/Higher (WS 18–20)

Nouns

Masculine		Feminine		Neuter	
der Bahnhof	railway station	die Altstadt	old town	das Fachwerkhaus	half-timbered house
der Busbahnhof	bus station	die Großstadt	large town, city	das Geschäft	business, shop
der Dom	cathedral	die Kirche	church		
der Ferienort	holiday destination	die Kleinstadt	small town	das Museum	museum
		die Landschaft	countryside, landscape	das Schloss	castle
der Flughafen	airport			das Sportzentrum	sports centre
der Laden	shop	die Sportmöglichkeit	sports facility	das Stadion	stadium
der Marktplatz	market place	die Stadtmitte	town centre		

Verbs and useful expressions

donnerstags	on Thursdays	Mittwoch, Donnerstag, Freitag, Samstag (Sonnabend), Sonntag	Wednesday, Thursday, Friday, Saturday, Sunday
freitags	on Fridays		
die ganze Familie	the whole family		
gefallen (+ dative):	to please:		
es gefällt mir	I like it	montags	on Mondays
geöffnet	open	nicht einmal	not even
geschlossen	shut	ein paar	a few
es gibt nichts/viel	there's nothing/lots	sonntags	on Sundays
für Jugendliche	for young people	uninteressant	uninteresting
hässlich	ugly	an Wochenenden	at weekends
(höchst) langweilig	(extremely) boring	wunderschön	really beautiful
Montag, Dienstag,	Monday, Tuesday,	ziemlich	quite, rather

Try learning vocabulary like this: read it, cover it, say it, uncover it and check it.

Transport and finding the way
◆ Foundation and ◆ ◆ Foundation/Higher (WS 24–26)

Nouns

Masculine		Feminine		Neuter	
der D-Zug	express train	die Autobahn	motorway	das Flugzeug	aeroplane ('fly-thing')
der Eingang	entrance	die (Bus)haltestelle	(bus) stop		
der Fahrkarten-schalter	ticket window	die Fahrkarte	ticket	das Geld	money
		die (erste/zweite) Klasse	(first/second) class	das Krankenhaus	hospital
der Flughafen	airport			das Spielzeug	toy(s), plaything(s)
der Imbiss	snack	die Reise	journey		
der InterCity-Zug	Intercity train	die Straßenbahn	tram		
der Nahverkehr	local traffic	die Stube	room		
der (Not)ausgang	(emergency) exit	die Tankstelle	petrol station		
der Zug	train				

Verbs and useful expressions

abfahren	to leave
Achtung!	be careful, watch out!
(pünktlich) ankommen	to arrive (punctually)
hin und zurück	return
hinter (dem/der/dem)	behind (the)
mit dem (Bus/Zug)	by (bus/train)
neben (dem/der/dem)	next to (the)
vor (dem/der/dem)	in front of (the)
warten auf	to wait for

If you learn the masculine, feminine and neuter words in separate lists you're less likely to get the genders wrong!

Name/
Group:

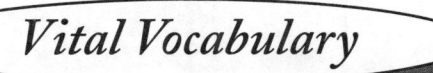

Vital Vocabulary

Home and local environment
◆ ◆ ◆ Higher (WS 21)

Nouns

Masculine		Feminine		Neuter	
der Aufzug	*lift*	die Apotheke	*chemist's, pharmacy*	das Blumenbeet	*flower bed*
der Balkon	*balcony*	die Bushaltestelle	*bus stop*	das Einkaufszentrum	*shopping centre*
der Baum	*tree*	die Gegend	*area*		
der Neubau	*modern block of flats*	die Grundschule	*primary school*	das Familienmitglied	*family member*
		die Klinik	*clinic, surgery*	das Gebäude	*building*
		die Ordnung	*order(liness)*	das Kleinkind	*toddler*
der Rasen	*lawn*	die Stadtmitte	*town centre*	das Spielzeug	*toy(s)*
der Traum	*dream*	die Treppe	*stairs, staircase*	das Stockwerk	*storey, floor*
		die Wäscheleine	*washing line*		

Verbs and useful expressions

außer Betrieb	*out of order*
hinaufsteigen	*to go up, climb up*
nötig	*necessary*
am Rande	*on the edge*
ruhig	*quiet*
sparen	*to save*
eines Tages	*one day*
nicht weit von	*not far from*
zufrieden	*contented, happy*

A good way to fix things in your mind is to go through them last thing at night. Zzzzzz!

Transport and finding the way
◆ ◆ ◆ Higher (WS 27)

Rewrite your wordlists with different words at the beginning and end each time. That way you'll learn them better, because the first and the last words are the easiest to remember!

Nouns

Masculine

der Kraftstoff	*fuel*
der Tagesausflug	*day trip*
der Urlaub	*holiday, leave*
der Weltraum	*space*

Feminine

die Technik	*technology*
die Umwelt	*environment*
die Zeit	*time*
die Zukunft	*future*

Neuter

(das) Ägypten	*Egypt*
das Raum-Fahrrad	*space-bike*
das Raumschiff	*spaceship*
das Zentrum	*centre*

Verbs and useful expressions

anderswohin	*(to) somewhere else*
belasten	*to put pressure on*
dauern	*to last*
deshalb	*therefore, so*
dorthin	*(to) there*
hingehen	*to go (there)*
künstlich	*artificial*
lösen	*to solve*
Urlaub machen	*to go on holiday*
verreisen	*to travel, go away*

Name/
Group:

Hotel	Ausstattung
A Münchner Kurhotel	Zimmer mit Bad und Klimaanlage, Schwimmbad, Fitnessraum, Segelsport, ruhig gelegen
B Pension Zum Löwen	Zimmer mit Bad und Telefon, Tennisplatz, Kegelbahn, Hotelrestaurant, Hotelbar
C Hotel Oberammergau	Zimmer mit Toilette und Dusche, behindertengerecht, Hunde willkommen, kinderfreundlich
D Bayerischer Hof	Zimmer mit Dusche, Aufzug, Parkhaus, Sauna, Solarium, Diätspeisen auf Anfrage

Some of these hotels don't take dogs ...

1 Look at the information and pick hotels for the people below.
(5 marks)

Beispiel:
Sigrid wants a hotel with a lift, and an indoor car park for her classic car. [D]

1 Björn wants a hotel with a gym, and also air conditioning in his room. ☐

2 Heike wants a hotel that takes pets and children. ☐

3 Oliver wants a room with a bath in a hotel that has a skittle alley. ☐

4 Dennis is disabled and wants a room with a toilet and a shower. ☐

5 Arno is on a special diet and wants a hotel with a sauna. ☐

... but are there any that don't take humans?!

Clever clues

➤ As usual with any German text, look for words or parts of words that you already know. It might help to note them down – in this text there are lots of them.

➤ Now work out what other parts of the words mean. For instance, **Fitness** is obvious, and what does **raum** look or sound like (Hotel A)?

➤ You may need a bit of help with **Klimaanlage** (Hotel A). If you change the 'k' to a 'c', **Klima** looks a bit like … what? So what is it connected with? What might you find in a hotel room in this context?

➤ Don't mix up our old friends **Segel** and **Kegel** (Hotels A & B)!

➤ In English we often put '-friendly' on the end of words (e.g. 'environmentally-friendly'). Well, German does the same. So what's **kinderfreundlich** (Hotel C)?

If you're still stuck, look up the words in the *Vital Vocabulary* (worksheet 38) – but make sure you don't forget them again! It's a good idea to keep a list of words you didn't know but have looked up.

1 Schreib den richtigen Buchstaben in jedes Kästchen. (5 marks)

Beispiel:
Die Toilette ist kaputt! `G`

1 Das Licht funktioniert nicht! ☐

2 Es gibt keine Handtücher in meinem Zimmer! ☐

3 Die Nachbarn machen zu viel Lärm! ☐

4 Das Zimmer ist zu kalt! ☐

5 Der Fernseher ist kaputt! ☐

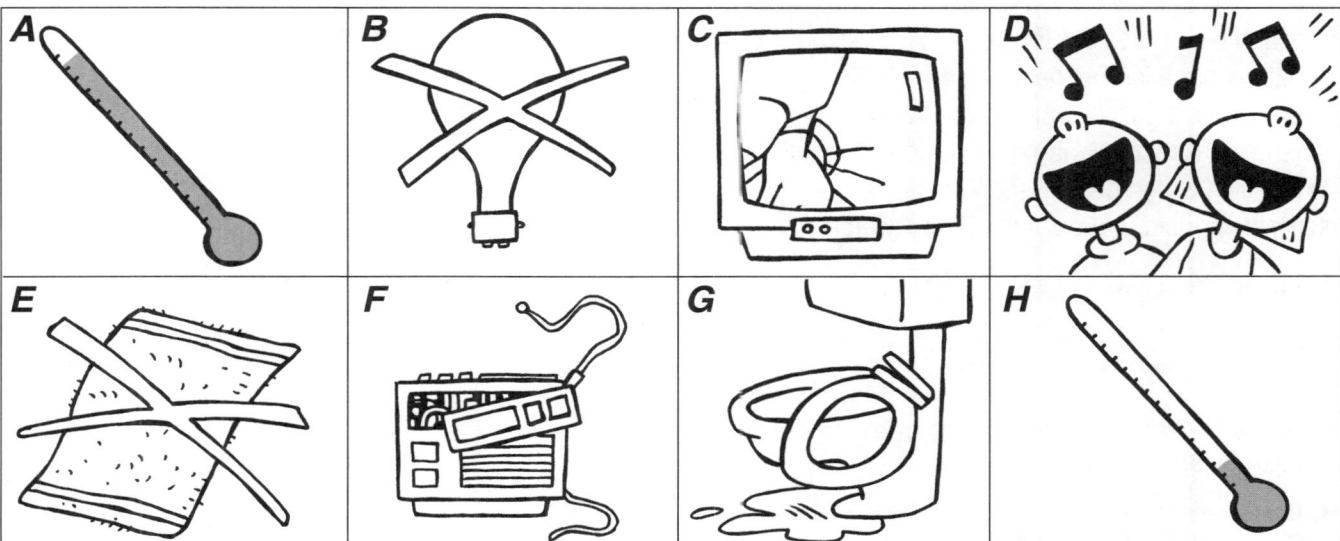

> With hotels like those, I'm happy to spend my time 'in the dog house' ...

Clever clues

➤ Don't forget to check for **negatives** – some of these complaints use negative expressions like **nicht** or **kein**, but others just talk about too much of something.

➤ **Kaputt** (Beispiel) is a useful word to learn – you may be able to use it in writing and speaking tasks. Can you find another way of saying the same thing in the texts?

➤ **Handtücher** (sentence 2) is made up of two words – **Hand** is obvious, but the other bit isn't! So what could it be that you find in hotel rooms and use for your hands? It can't be soap: that's not in the pictures.

➤ What English words are **Licht** (sentence 1) and **Nachbar(n)** (sentence 3) similar to?

Finally, don't forget the *Vital Vocabulary* (worksheet 38) if you need a safety net!

Name/
Group:

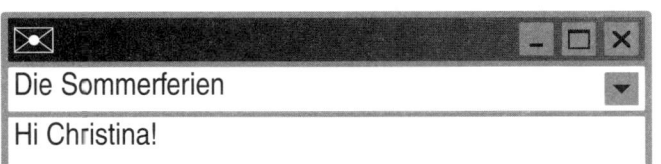

Die Sommerferien

Hi Christina!

Wie waren deine Sommerferien? Meine waren ätzend! Ich habe drei Wochen mit meiner Familie an der Nordseeküste in der Nähe von Rostock verbracht. Wir sind mit dem Auto dorthin gefahren und unterwegs war das Wetter viel zu heiß. Ich musste den Rücksitz mit meiner kleinen Schwester teilen und ich finde sie nervig. In Rostock hat es drei Wochen lang geregnet. Es war so langweilig. Meistens habe ich Bücher gelesen oder ferngesehen – ich bin nicht geschwommen und wir haben nur einen (regnerischen!) Tag am Strand verbracht! Hoffentlich waren deine Ferien etwas besser – schreib mir bald und sag mir, wie sie waren!

Viele Grüße
Fredi

☞ Handy hints

➤ Don't forget where to look for both parts of verbs in the perfect tense. If you see any auxiliary verbs (**bin, sind, habe(n)**, etc.), look at the **end** of the sentence for the **past participle**. It's important because it gives you more information than the auxiliary.

➤ Look for **context clues**. Fredi says his holidays were **ätzend**. If you don't know what this means, read the rest of the text and it becomes pretty clear what kind of holiday he had …

➤ Look for examples of the same or a similar idea expressed in different ways in the text and in the questions, e.g. **nur einen Tag** and **sehr wenig Zeit** (Qu 5).

1 Schreib **R** (richtig), **F** (falsch) oder **?** (nicht im Text).
(5 marks)

Beispiel:
Fredi hat die Sommerferien toll gefunden. [F]

1 Unterwegs war es sehr heiß. ☐

2 Er ist mit dem Zug nach Rostock gefahren. ☐

3 Seine Mutter geht ihm auf die Nerven. ☐

4 In Rostock war das Wetter heiß und sonnig. ☐

5 Er hat sehr wenig Zeit am Strand verbracht. ☐

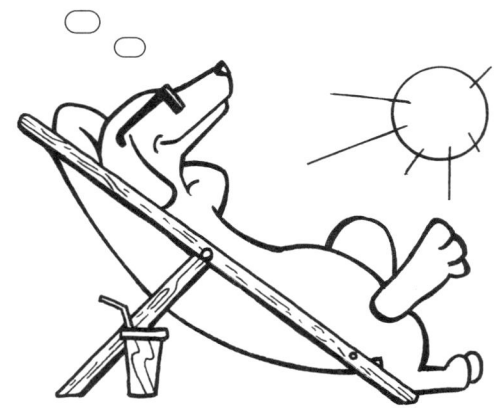

Name/
Group:

Wie findest du Weihnachten?

Wir haben mit zwei Jugendlichen aus Bremen gesprochen und sie gefragt, wie sie Weihnachten finden. Unsere Frage: „Seid ihr Weihnachtsfans oder würdet ihr das Weihnachtsfest am liebsten ausfallen lassen?" Hier sind ihre Antworten:

Ich bin ein absoluter Weihnachtsfan. Ich mag einfach die Atmosphäre in der Weihnachtszeit. Alle Geschäfte und die Innenstädte sind festlich geschmückt. Und am besten finde ich die Weihnachtsmärkte. Dort kann man sich mit Freunden treffen und etwas Heißes trinken. Und überall riecht es nach Schoko-Nüssen, Lebkuchen und Bratwürstchen. Ich finde das total schön.

Kirsten, 16, Stuttgart

Ich würde meiner Familie vorschlagen, die Geschenke einfach wegzulassen oder nur ganz kleine Geschenke zu machen. Das wäre dann viel weniger Stress. Und das Geld könnte man dann entweder sparen oder für einen guten Zweck spenden. Denn ich finde, eigentlich hat ja jeder schon alles und man braucht wirklich nicht noch ein Parfüm oder noch mehr Schokolade.

Anke, 17, Ulm

Tips for texts

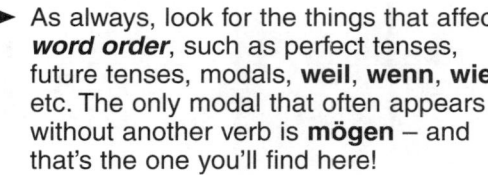
➤ As always, look for the things that affect ***word order***, such as perfect tenses, future tenses, modals, **weil**, **wenn**, **wie**, etc. The only modal that often appears without another verb is **mögen** – and that's the one you'll find here!

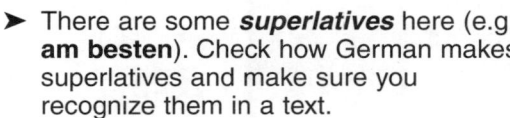
➤ There are some ***superlatives*** here (e.g. **am besten**). Check how German makes superlatives and make sure you recognize them in a text.

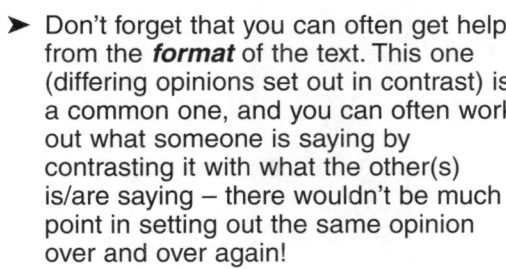
➤ Don't forget that you can often get help from the ***format*** of the text. This one (differing opinions set out in contrast) is a common one, and you can often work out what someone is saying by contrasting it with what the other(s) is/are saying – there wouldn't be much point in setting out the same opinion over and over again!

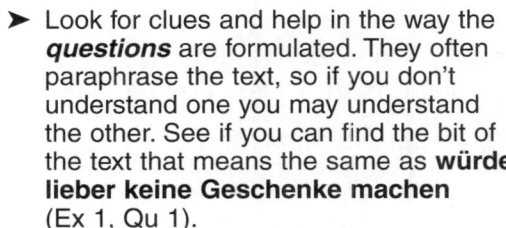
➤ Look for clues and help in the way the ***questions*** are formulated. They often paraphrase the text, so if you don't understand one you may understand the other. See if you can find the bit of the text that means the same as **würde lieber keine Geschenke machen** (Ex 1, Qu 1).

➤ Do you know how to use the ***conditional***? This verb form is used to say 'would', 'could', 'should', 'might', etc. Conditionals appear in several of the questions here, so you need to be able to recognize them.

---

1 Lies den Text. (5 marks)
Wer …

Beispiel:
… findet Weihnachten wirklich supertoll?   *Kirsten*

1 … würde lieber keine Geschenke machen? _____

2 … möchte das Geld z.B. Hilfsorganisationen geben? _____

3 … trifft sich gern mit Freunden auf dem Weihnachtsmarkt? _____

4 … mag den Geruch von Weihnachten gern? _____

5 … findet, Weihnachtsgeschenke will meistens keiner haben? _____

2 Lies den Text noch einmal und wähl entweder A, B, C oder D. (3 marks)

Beispiel: Kirsten besucht sehr gern
A Weihnachtsmärkte **B** Schulen
C Drogerien **D** ihre Großmutter. [A]

1 Anke würde lieber **A** riesige Geschenke **B** Haustiere **C** kleinere Geschenke **D** Bonbons verschenken. ☐

2 Ankes Meinung nach braucht man **A** Lebkuchen **B** mehr Geschenke **C** viele Schoko-Nüsse **D** nicht noch mehr Schokolade. ☐

3 Kirstens Einstellung zu Weihnachten ist **A** gelangweilt **B** begeistert **C** gleichgültig **D** extrem negativ. ☐

Name/
Group:

LILLIS IMBISS

LECKEREIEN

Käsetoast	5,75 €
Gulaschsuppe mit Speck	3,25 €
Heringsfilet	6,25 €
Bockwurst	3,00 €
Grüner Salat	4,50 €
mit Senf oder Majonäse	nach Wunsch

NACHSPEISEN

2 Kugeln Eis nach Wunsch	3,25 €
mit Vanillesoße oder Sahne	+0,25 €

FÜR UNSERE KLEINEN GÄSTE

Hähnchen Croccies	
mit Pommes frites	4,25 €

HEISSE GETRÄNKE

Kännchen Kaffee	2,00 €
Glas schwarzer Tee	1,00 €

ALKOHOLFREIE GETRÄNKE

Coca-Cola	1,50 €
Sprite	1,50 €

ALKOHOLISCHE GETRÄNKE

Bier vom Fass 0,3 l	1,75 €
Weißwein:	
Riesling halbtrocken	2,25 €
Rotwein:	
Beaujolais trocken	2,75 €

Yuck! I ordered 'Bockwurst mit Sahne' instead of 'mit Senf'!

1 You're on holiday in Germany with your family, and you visit a snack bar. Your parents don't speak German, so you need to help them understand the menu. Answer the questions.

1 Your mum's a vegetarian and doesn't eat fish – which TWO savoury items could she eat? (2 marks) _____

2 Your little sister wants the kids' menu – what kind of meat will she have? (1 mark) _____

3 How many fish items are there on the menu? (1 mark) _____

4 Your dad wants coffee – will he get a cup or a pot for 2 euros? (1 mark) _____

5 After he's paid the bill, your dad decides he wants a sausage as well. The trouble is, he only has 3.50 euros left – can he afford it? (1 mark) _____

Clever clues

➤ Menus usually have lots of clues. First, there's the *order* things are in: usually savoury things or snacks, followed by main courses, desserts and drinks. The 'wild card' is if there's a children's menu – where is that here?

➤ Now look for *cognates* or *near-cognates* (words that are the same, or nearly the same, in English and German). Menus are usually full of them, because a lot of food words come from English or American, or originally from French.

➤ Some words *look* different from the English, but *sound* very similar. If you split **Gulaschsuppe** into two, the first part sounds exactly like the same word in English and the second part sounds similar to its English equivalent.

➤ Make sure you know your sauces! You don't want to get cream on your sausages like our friend – and you don't want mustard on your ice-cream, either.

➤ Look for clues in the *questions*. The first question asks for *two* vegetarian items, so find them by a process of elimination.

Don't forget that the *Vital Vocabulary* (worksheet 38) is there to help you.

Name/
Group:

Die Wettervorhersage

München windig; teilweise sonnig
Hamburg stürmisch mit Schneeschauern
Frankfurt kalt und neblig
Berlin heiter bis wolkig
Dresden am Morgen Regen; später sonnig

> Funny how the German word for weather starts with 'Wet'!

1 Schreib den Namen der richtigen Stadt auf. (4 marks)

 A

 B

 C

Beispiel: _Berlin_ _____ _____

 D

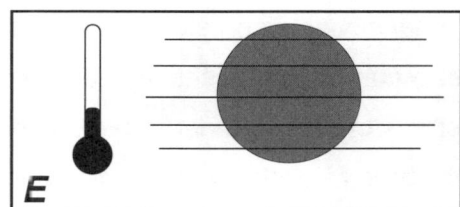 E

_____ _____

Clever clues

➤ Get as much information as you can from pictures, titles and so on.

➤ **Word endings** in English often have an equivalent in German. A good example in the text is the words for 'sunny' and 'stormy'. Which *two* adjective endings in German are the equivalent of '-y' on the end of an English adjective?

➤ Don't forget to *say* the words to yourself. **Schauer** (Hamburg) may look unfamiliar, but if you say it, it sounds almost exactly like its English equivalent.

➤ Sometimes words *look* similar as well. **Stürmisch** (Hamburg) looks a bit like the English if you replace the **-isch** on the end with its English equivalent ending.

➤ Look for **compound words** that consist of two easy words joined together to make a hard (looking!) one. **Schneeschauer** (Hamburg) is just **Schnee** and **Schauer** joined up, and those are both very similar to their English equivalents.

Use the *Vital Vocabulary* (worksheet 38) to make sure you know all the weather expressions by heart, not just the easy ones!

Name/
Group:

Ich habe meinen Mantel im Zug liegen lassen. Ich weiß nicht genau wann, aber es war irgendwann am Montagmorgen, 24. Juli. Der Mantel ist ziemlich klein (Größe 28, und ist aus braunem Leder (sehr wertvoll!). Die Marke ist Krokodil. Mein Reisepass und mein Führerschein waren in der Tasche.

Anja Schlesser

Ich habe meinen Mantel irgendwo verloren. Ich habe keine Ahnung, wo das war, aber vielleicht im Park oder in der Nähe vom Busbahnhof. Es war am 18. August um ungefähr acht Uhr morgens. Der Mantel ist braun und aus Leder, und die Größe ist 32 oder so (ich bin nicht ganz sicher!). Dreißig Euro und meine Kreditkarten waren in der Tasche.

Melanie Dillinger

Ich habe meinen Regenmantel irgendwo im Flughafen liegen lassen. Ich weiß nicht genau wo, aber vielleicht in der Nähe des Fahrkarten-schalters – ich bin nicht sicher. Der Mantel ist braun und war ziemlich billig. Die Größe ist 44 und in der Tasche waren einige Bonbons und ein Foto von meinem Freund.

Judith Galland

1 *Im Fundbüro:* Wer ist das? Lies die Sätze und schreib „Anja", „Melanie" oder „Judith" auf. (5 marks)

Beispiel: Sie weiß nicht genau, welche Größe ihr Mantel hat.　　　*Melanie*

1　Sie ist nicht total sicher, wann sie ihren Mantel liegen lassen hat.　　_____

2　Ihr Mantel ist braun und hat nicht viel gekostet.　　_____

3　Ihr Mantel ist aus braunem Leder und die Größe ist ungefähr zweiunddreißig.　　_____

4　In der Tasche ihres Mantels waren etwas Geld und einige Kreditkarten.　　_____

5　Sie hat ihren Mantel wahrscheinlich im Flughafen liegen lassen.　　_____

👉 Handy hints

➤ Look for **tense clues**: anything about lost property is going to have some perfect tenses, giving details of when and where the item was lost, etc.

➤ Look for **adjectives** and make a list of them if it helps. The adjectives here mostly come *after* their nouns – what effect does that have on them?

➤ Look for how to say what **material** something is made of. This is in fact similar to the way English does it, but it's easy to miss.

➤ As these texts are about things that people have lost and haven't got any more, there are some **negatives** here. **Ich habe keine Ahnung** (Melanie) is a useful phrase – can you work out what it means?

➤ Some words for characteristics, like **Marke**, are similar to the English. However, **Größe** isn't – but what German word is it like?

FUNDBÜRO

Name/
Group:

Nürnberg

Wer die Architektur des Mittelalters mag, der ist in Nürnberg richtig. Über der Stadt thront die mittelalterliche Burg, die heute ein Museum ist. In der Nürnberger Innenstadt kann man sich die historischen Gebäude und den Brunnen am Markt anschauen oder auch ausgiebig shoppen gehen.

In Nürnberg gibt es auch etwas für Eisenbahn-Fans: Hier findet man das DB-Museum, das Firmenmuseum der Deutschen Bahn. Das Museum wurde kurz vor Anfang des zwanzigsten Jahrhunderts gegründet und ist damit eines der ältesten Eisenbahnmuseen in Europa. Hier gibt es auch etwas für Kinder: das Nürnberger Spielzeugmuseum. Das Museum liegt im Herzen der Nürnberger Altstadt und hat als Schwerpunkt die beiden letzten Jahrhunderte.

Es gibt auch zwei Nürnberger Spezialitäten, die weltbekannt sind: Bratwürstchen und Lebkuchen. Nürnberger Bratwürstchen sind klein und dünn und im Restaurant bekommt man zwölf Stück pro Portion zusammen mit Sauerkraut. Nürnberger Lebkuchen sind ein Gebäck mit vielen Gewürzen und Honig, das besonders in der Weihnachtszeit gegessen wird.

Tips for texts

➤ *Word order* is always one of the biggest issues in a German text. Here, look at what **wer** in the first sentence does to the verb it's with.

➤ Which word is used in German to mean 'that' or 'which'? It's similar in form to a very common word you'll have learnt very early on. And, of course, it sends the verb to the end!

➤ Remember to look for clues in the *questions*. When the questions are in German, it's quite likely that parts of them will *paraphrase* the things in the text they are asking about, so you have a second chance. If you didn't understand **Eisenbahn** in this text, you probably do know **Züge** in Ex 1 Qu 1.

---

1 Beantworte die Fragen. (4 marks)

Beispiel: Was kann man sich in der Nürnberger Innenstadt anschauen?

> *Die historischen Gebäude und den Brunnen am Markt*

1 Was gibt es in Nürnberg für Leute, die sich für Züge interessieren?

_____

2 In welchem Stadtteil befindet sich das Nürnberger Spielzeugmuseum?

_____

3 Wie sieht ein Nürnberger Bratwürstchen aus?

_____

4 Zu welcher Jahreszeit isst man normalerweise Nürnberger Lebkuchen?

_____

2 Lies den Text noch einmal und wähl entweder A, B, C oder D. (4 marks)

Beispiel: In Nürnberg ist
A die Burg **B** der Bahnhof
C der Brunnen **D** die Innenstadt
jetzt ein Museum. ☐ A

1 Kinder interessieren sich besonders für
A den Bahnhof **B** den Brunnen
C das Spielzeugmuseum **D** die Burg. ☐

2 In der Nürnberger Innenstadt kann man
A windsurfen **B** shoppen
C schwimmen **D** Ski fahren
gehen. ☐

3 Das Eisenbahnmuseum wurde im
A 18. **B** 19. **C** 20. **D** 21.
Jahrhundert eröffnet. ☐

4 Man isst normalerweise
A zwei **B** zehn **C** zwölf **D** zwanzig
Nürnberger Bratwürstchen auf einmal. ☐

Name/
Group:

Vital Vocabulary

Tourism and accommodation
◆ Foundation and
◆◆ Foundation/Higher (WS 30–32)

Holiday activities and services
◆ Foundation and
◆◆ Foundation/Higher (WS 34–36)

Nouns

Masculine

der Aufzug	lift
der Fernseher	television set
der Fitnessraum	fitness/exercise room, gym
der Lärm	noise
der Nachbar/ die Nachbarin	neighbour
der (Rück)sitz	(back) seat
der Segelsport	sailing (as a sport)
der Strand	beach
der Tennisplatz	tennis court

Feminine

die Ausstattung	facilities
die Dusche	shower
die Kegelbahn	skittle alley
die Klimaanlage	air conditioning
die Nordseeküste	North Sea coast
die Pension	guest house; full board

Neuter

das Bad	bath
das Handtuch	towel
das Kurhotel	spa hotel
das Licht	light
das Parkhaus	covered parking
das Schwimmbad	swimming pool
das Wetter	weather
das Zimmer	room

Plural

die Diätspeisen	diet foods
die Sommerferien	summer holidays

Verbs and useful expressions

auf Anfrage	on request
ätzend	awful
behindertengerecht	accessible to disabled people
dorthin	(to) there
drei Wochen lang	(for) three weeks
funktionieren	to work, function
heiß	hot
kalt	cold
kaputt	broken, out of order
kinderfreundlich	child-friendly
lesen	to read
müssen	to have to, 'must'
in der Nähe von	near
nervig	irritating
regnen	to rain
ruhig gelegen	quietly situated
sonnig	sunny
teilen	share
unterwegs	on the way
verbracht	spent

Nouns

Masculine

der Führerschein	driving licence
(der) grüner Salat	green salad, lettuce
der Käsetoast	cheese on toast
der Mantel	coat
der Regen	rain
der Regenmantel	raincoat, mac
der Reisepass	passport
der (Schnee)schauer	(snow) shower
der Senf	mustard
der Speck	bacon

Feminine

die Bockwurst	boiled sausage
die Größe	size
die Gulaschsuppe	goulash soup
die Kugel	scoop (of ice-cream)
die Marke	trade name, label, marque
die Nachspeise	dessert
die Sahne	cream
die Tasche	pocket
die Wettervorhersage	weather forecast

Neuter

das Fass (vom Fass)	barrel (on draught)
das Hähnchen	chicken
das Heringsfilet	herring fillet
das Kännchen	small pot

Plural

die Bonbons	sweets
die Getränke	drinks
die Leckereien	(tasty) snacks
die Pommes frites	chips, fries

Verbs and useful expressions

keine Ahnung haben	to have no idea
alkoholfrei	alcohol-free, soft
alkoholisch	alcoholic
aus (Stoff/Leder)	made of (cloth/leather)
heiter bis wolkig	pleasant to cloudy
irgendwann/irgendwo	some time/somewhere
liegen lassen	to leave behind
nach Wunsch	to taste
neblig	foggy
regnerisch	rainy
später	later
stürmisch	stormy
teilweise	partly
ungefähr	about
wertvoll	valuable
zu viel	too much

You could colour-code nouns by gender, to help you remember whether they're masculine, feminine or neuter.

Try learning vocabulary against the clock: how many items can you learn in a 10-minute burst?

Name/ Group:

As the exam approaches, you'll need all the vocabulary help you can get. Try putting lists of words to learn on the wall in funny places! That way they will always be around you – and perhaps other family members will learn them and remind you as well!

Tourism and accommodation
◆ ◆ ◆ Higher (WS 33)

Nouns

Masculine

der Lebkuchen	*spicy gingerbread*
der Weihnachtsfan	*fan of Christmas*
der Weihnachtsmarkt	*Christmas market*
der (gute) Zweck	*(good) cause, purpose*

Feminine

die Atmosphäre	*atmosphere*
die Innenstadt	*town centre ('inner town')*
die Schoko-Nuss	*chocolate nut*
die Weihnachtszeit	*Christmas time*

Neuter

das Bratwürstchen	*small grilled sausage*
das Geschenk	*present*
das Parfüm	*perfume*
das Weihnachtsfest	*Christmas festival*

Plural

Weihnachten	*Christmas*

Verbs and useful expressions

absolut	*absolute(ly)*
ausfallen lassen	*to do away with*
brauchen	*to need*
eigentlich	*actually*
einfach	*simply*
entweder … oder	*either … or*
etwas Heißes	*something hot*
festlich geschmückt	*festively decorated*
Geschenke machen	*to exchange presents*
jeder	*each, every(body)*
noch ein	*another*
riechen (nach)	*to smell (of)*
spenden	*to donate, give*
sich mit (Freunden) treffen	*to meet up with (friends)*
überall	*everywhere*
verschenken	*to give (a present)*
vorschlagen	*to suggest*
weglassen	*to leave out*
weniger	*less*

Holiday activities and services
◆ ◆ ◆ Higher (WS 37)

Nouns

Masculine

der Anfang	*beginning*
der Brunnen (am Markt)	*fountain (in the market place)*
der Eisenbahn-Fan	*train spotter, railway buff*
der Honig	*honey*
der Schwerpunkt	*focus*

Feminine

die Architektur	*architecture*
die Burg	*castle*
die Deutsche Bahn	*German Railways*
die Spezialität	*speciality*

Neuter

das Eisenbahnmuseum	*railway museum*
das Gebäck	*(piece of) baking, cake/biscuit*
das Gebäude	*building*
das Gewürz	*spice*
das Mittelalter	*the Middle Ages*
das Sauerkraut	*pickled cabbage*
das Spielzeugmuseum	*toy museum*
das (zwanzigste) Jahrhundert	*the (20th) century*

Verbs and useful expressions

sich (dat.) anschauen	*to look at*
sich befinden	*to be located*
gründen	*to found*
mittelalterlich	*medieval*
thronen (über)	*to preside, tower (over)*
weltbekannt	*world famous*

Some of these words don't really go together (honey and toy museums?!). But that can be a help: if you organize your words into topic lists, then alphabetical lists, etc., each time you write a new list you'll remember a few more words.

Name/
Group:

1 Am Schnellimbiss: Schreib den richtigen Buchstaben in jedes Kästchen. (5 marks)

Beispiel: Ich möchte einen Hamburger mit Senf. — C

1 Haben Sie heute Pommes frites? ☐

2 Was darf es sein? ☐

3 Ich möchte Senf dazu, bitte. ☐

4 Was für Würste haben Sie? ☐

5 Ich nehme eine Flasche Limo, bitte. ☐

A   B   C

D   E

F   G   H

2 Hier ist ein Einkaufszentrum in Deutschland. Schreib **R** (richtig), **F** (falsch) oder **?** (nicht im Text). (5 marks)

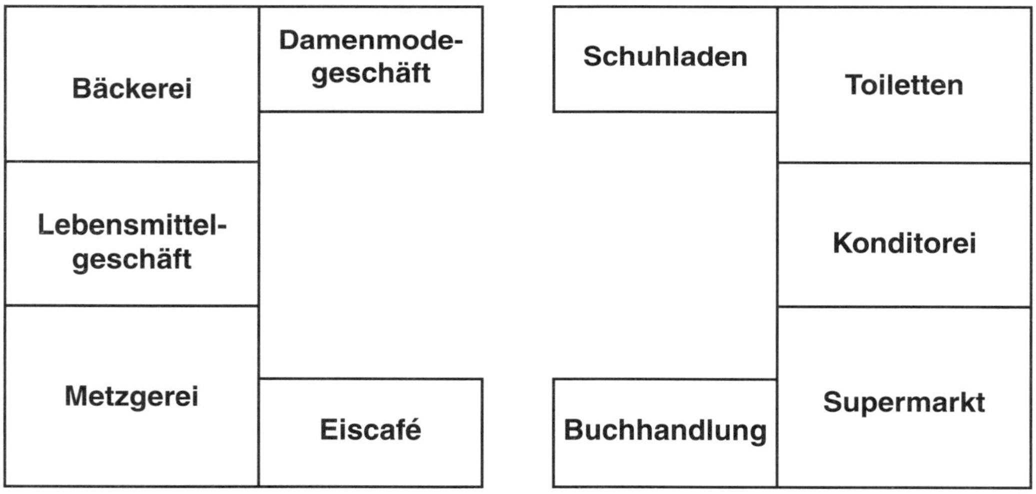

Bäckerei	Damenmodegeschäft	Schuhladen	Toiletten
Lebensmittelgeschäft			Konditorei
Metzgerei	Eiscafé	Buchhandlung	Supermarkt

Beispiel:

Die Bäckerei ist neben dem Damenmodegeschäft. — R

1 Das Lebensmittelgeschäft ist gegenüber der Konditorei. ☐

2 Die Buchhandlung ist hinter dem Eiscafé. ☐

3 Die Toiletten sind neben der Konditorei. ☐

4 Der Schuhladen ist gegenüber der Metzgerei. ☐

5 Die Metzgerei ist gegenüber dem Eiscafé. ☐

 Name/ Group:

1

Umweltfreundlicher Skiurlaub?

Es gibt in den Alpen in der Schweiz und in Österreich fast jeden Winter Lawinen und andere Naturkatastrophen – aber könnte man diese verhindern? Kann Wintersport umweltfreundlich sein? Mal sehen …

Skifahren in den Alpen bedeutet meistens tausende von Skitouristen und Skilifte, die die Skifahrer auf den Berg hinaufbringen, damit sie dann so schnell wie möglich wieder ins Tal fahren können. Diese Art des Skifahrens verursacht viele Probleme für die Umwelt. Es gibt aber viele Möglichkeiten, den Skiurlaub umweltfreundlicher zu gestalten. Zum Beispiel könnte man eine Fahrgemeinschaft bilden, d.h. das Auto mit Freunden teilen. Man kann auch die Natur respektieren und nur auf präparierten Pisten fahren. Beim Skifahren abseits der gekennzeichneten Pisten kann man nämlich leicht Lawinen auslösen.

Die dritte Möglichkeit, die Umwelt zu schonen, ist allerdings nicht so bequem! Beim Langlauf fährt man auf präparierten Wegen durch die Natur. Man steigt selbst kleine Berge hinauf, die man natürlich auch wieder hinunterfährt. Langlauf ist wie Joggen auf Skiern, allerdings nur bergauf. Bergab kann man mühelos gleiten und die Natur genießen.

1 Schreib den richtigen Buchstaben in jedes Kästchen. (4 marks)

Beispiel: Im Winter kann der Schnee in
A Frankreich B Österreich C Italien
D England
sehr gefährlich sein. ⬛ B

1 Wenn man im Winter in den Alpen Ski fahren geht, findet man oft tausende von
A Skitouristen B Flugzeugen
C Lawinen D Restaurants. ☐

2 Um den Skiurlaub umweltfreundlicher zu machen, könnte man A nicht dorthin fliegen B zu Hause bleiben C das Auto teilen D ein Fahrrad kaufen. ☐

3 Wenn man nicht auf den offiziellen Skipisten bleibt, kann man A sterben B Tiere töten C die Natur respektieren D Lawinen auslösen. ☐

4 Langlauf ist wie A Radfahren B Autofahren C Joggen D Fliegen auf Skiern. ☐

2

2 Make notes in English on the history of travel.

Beispiel: What began only 40 years ago?
  Charter flights to Mallorca

1 Which TWO countries did the fathers of organized travel come from? (2 marks)

2 What did Baedeker found in 1827? (1 mark)

3 Why were some air raids in the Second World War known as Baedeker raids? (1 mark)

4 What did Cook first organize in 1841? (1 mark)

5 When did Cook organize his first trip abroad? (1 mark)

Koffer packen und nichts wie weg!
Eine kurze Geschichte des Reisens

Heutzutage ist fast jeder Winkel der Welt mit Bahn, Schiff, Flugzeug und Auto problemlos zu erreichen. Das war aber nicht immer so. Die ersten Charterflüge nach Mallorca gab es zum Beispiel erst vor 40 Jahren. Hier sind die wichtigsten Eckdaten der etwa 170 Jahre alten Geschichte des Reisens.

Die Gründungsväter des organisierten Reisens waren der Deutsche Karl Baedeker und der Engländer Thomas Cook. Baedeker gründete 1827 in Koblenz eine Verlagsbuchhandlung und gab acht Jahre später seinen ersten Reiseführer heraus. Danach folgten unzählige „Baedeker"-Publikationen. Bombenangriffe während des Zweiten Weltkriegs auf schöne britische Städte nannte man sogar „Baedeker-Angriffe", weil die Städte im Baedeker-Reiseführer zu finden waren!

Der Engländer Thomas Cook fing etwa zur gleichen Zeit, nämlich 1841 an, die ersten Städtereisen zu organisieren. Etwas später, im Jahre 1855, organisierte Cook dann die erste Auslandsreise für Touristen. Der Reise zur Weltausstellung nach Paris folgten 1867 die Einführung von Reiseschecks und 1869 die erste Kreuzfahrt auf dem Nil.

Aber zum Schluss das wohl wichtigste Datum für viele Touristen: 1963 gab es den ersten Charterflug nach Mallorca. Es war die Geburtsstunde vom Pauschaltourismus: Flug, Unterkunft, Verpflegung und natürlich Sonne – alles war inklusive im Reise-Paket.

1 Schreib den richtigen Buchstaben in jedes Kästchen. (5 marks)

Beispiel:

Mein älterer Bruder wäscht immer das Auto. [H]

1 Meine Mutter mäht normalerweise den Rasen. ☐

2 Meine jüngere Schwester saugt am Wochenende Staub. ☐

3 Meine Großmutter spült abends ab. ☐

4 Mein Großvater deckt jeden Morgen den Tisch. ☐

5 Mein Vater macht ab und zu das Bett! ☐

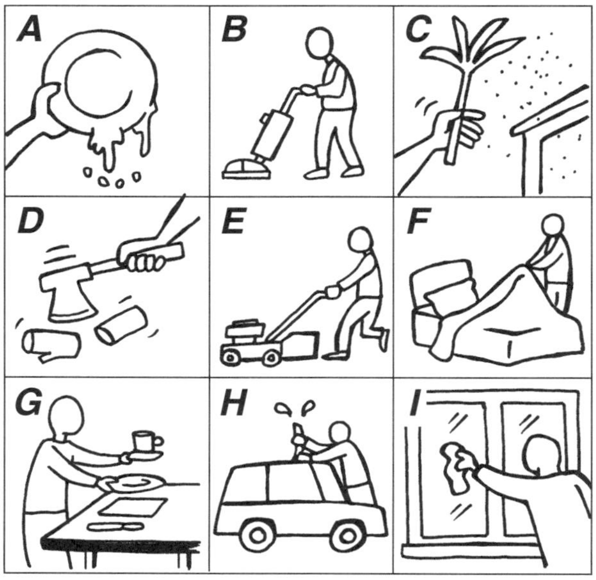

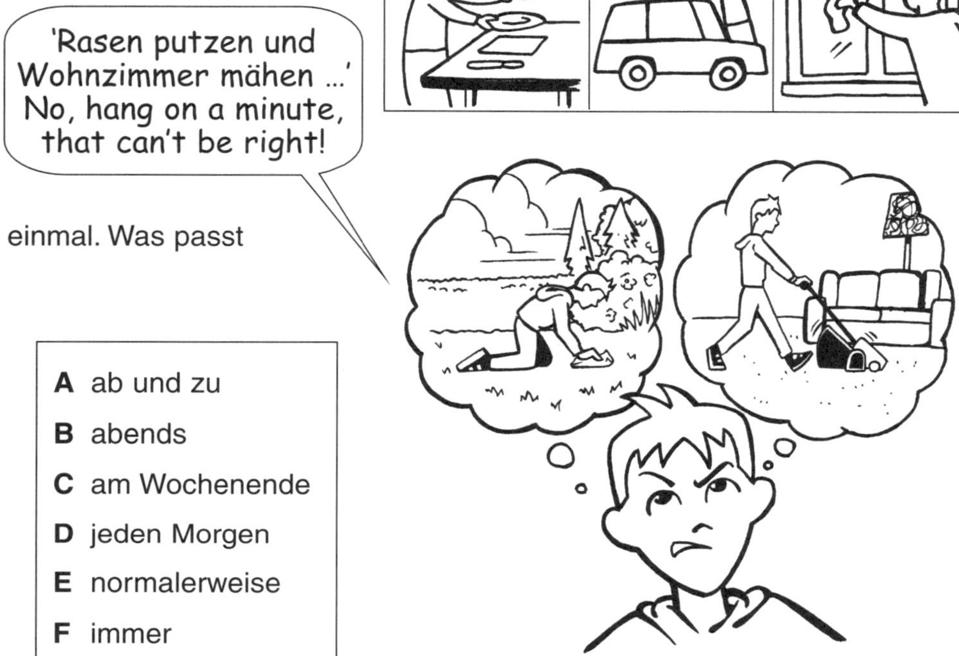

'Rasen putzen und Wohnzimmer mähen ...' No, hang on a minute, that can't be right!

2 Lies die Sätze oben noch einmal. Was passt zusammen? (5 marks)

Beispiel:

[F]

1 ☐

2 ☐

3 ☐

4 ☐

5 ☐

A ab und zu
B abends
C am Wochenende
D jeden Morgen
E normalerweise
F immer

Clever clues

➤ Look for **time and frequency** words: whenever people are talking about *who* does *what* and *when*, there will be frequency words. How many can you find here?

➤ Several of the words for chores (like **abspülen**, sentence 3) are **separable verbs**. Don't forget to look for the other half of the verb at the **end** of the sentence.

➤ If you don't know **spült ab**, use logic: **abends** tells you it's a chore that you do in the evenings ...

➤ Look for clues in the pictures: only two pictures show a **Tisch** (sentence 4) and a **Bett** (sentence 5).

Last but not least, don't forget the *Vital Vocabulary* (worksheet 50) if you need to check any chores or time words.

Name/
Group:

1 Was gibt's zum Frühstück? Wähl die passenden Wörter. (5 marks)

Beispiel:
H

1 ☐

2 ☐

3 ☐

4 ☐

5 ☐

A	Cornflakes
B	Käse
C	Kaffee
D	Milch
E	Erdbeerkonfitüre
F	Brötchen
G	Schinken
H	Apfelsaft
I	Tee
J	Müsli

Clever clues

➤ Don't forget *cultural clues*. If you know what people in German-speaking countries have for breakfast, you'll find this exercise a lot easier. It's no good looking for bacon, fried eggs and fried bread!

➤ Most of these words are 'singles': there aren't many compound words (words made up from more than one other word). But make sure you know **Konfitüre** (E) and **Saft** (H), because they often appear as part of compounds.

➤ *Suffixes* are useful clues. **-chen** on the end of a word tells you it's 'little', and you have to put an **Umlaut** (¨) on the vowel before it. So what is a **Brötchen** (F), literally?

2 Was isst Markus zum Abendessen?
Füll die Tabelle aus.

und abends essen wir um halb sieben. Ich esse meistens Brot mit Salami und Käse, und als Nachtisch gibt es normalerweise Jogurt und Obst. Ich trinke immer ein Glas Milch. Und du? Was isst du normalerweise zu Abend?

Schreib bald zurück. Bis bald!

Markus

Clever clues

➤ Look for *key words* in Markus' description of his evening meal. **Salami** is like the English, but what are the other two savoury items he mentions?

➤ You should be able to recognize **Jogurt**, and if you didn't know **Obst**, think of something you can eat with yoghurt!

Finally, don't forget your usual trawl through the *Vital Vocabulary* (worksheet 50) for any words you don't know – and to reinforce the ones you do!

Beispiel:

Hauptspeise	*Brot*			(2 marks)
Nachtisch				(2 marks)
Getränk				(1 mark)

Name/
Group:

I heard that Essen was a big town in Germany. Strange name for a town – 'Eating'!

Gesund essen kann *Spaß* machen!

Wenn man gesund essen will, ist es besser nicht immer im Supermarkt einzukaufen. Man kann auch auf den Markt gehen und dort frisches Gemüse, Obst, Fleisch und Eier kaufen. Das ist vielleicht etwas teurer und dauert vielleicht auch etwas länger, aber es ist gesund und macht mehr Spaß.

Es ist auch besser, mehr aus dem Essen zu machen, sich zum Essen hinzusetzen und sich aufs Essen zu konzentrieren. Am besten isst man nur dann, wenn man wirklich etwas essen will.

7 Schreib **R** (richtig), **F** (falsch) oder **?** (nicht im Text). (5 marks)

Beispiel:

Um gesund zu essen kauft man am besten im Supermarkt ein. ☐ F

1 Man kann im Supermarkt billiger als auf dem Markt einkaufen. ☐

2 Auf dem Markt kann man normalerweise Reis kaufen. ☐

3 Frische Produkte vom Markt sind gesund. ☐

4 Wenn man isst, ist es besser, so oft wie möglich aufzustehen. ☐

5 Es ist besser, nur zu essen, wenn man wirklich Hunger hat. ☐

👉 Handy hints

➤ There are some *modal* verbs and *subordinate clauses* here, which change the word order, so look at the ends of sentences for key words.

➤ You should be familiar with **superlatives** by now ('best', 'biggest', etc.), but in this text there are some *comparatives*. As the text is saying where you can buy things 'more cheaply', eat 'more healthily', etc., it will be useful if you can identify them. See how many you can list and write down their meanings.

➤ The phrase **Spaß machen** is a common one – what does it mean?

Don't forget to check the *Vital Vocabulary* (worksheet 50) if you're still stuck!

Name/
Group:

Sollte man aufhören Fleisch zu essen, und Vegetarier werden? Oder ist das eine verrückte Idee? Wir haben vier Jugendliche gefragt, was sie von vegetarischer Ernährung halten.

KONTRA   **Michaela**, 18

Ich bin absolut gegen vegetarische Ernährung. Der Mensch ist nun mal kein Vegetarier. Und was die Vegetarier so essen, schmeckt doch scheußlich. Ich habe neulich mal so eine Tofu-Wurst probiert. Die hat nach absolut gar nichts geschmeckt. Ich kann mir nicht vorstellen, wie ein Mensch auf diese Weise leben kann …

PRO   **Janina**, 17

Vegetarische Ernährung finde ich gut. Ich bin selber Vegetarierin, esse aber Milchprodukte und Eier. Ich finde, dass man in der heutigen Zeit einfach nicht mehr mit ruhigem Gewissen Fleisch essen kann. Fleisch zu essen ist schlecht für die Umwelt – und auch schlecht für die Tiere, die getötet werden!

KONTRA   **Wiebke**, 16

Für mich wäre es unmöglich, ohne Fleisch zu leben. Ich finde, Fleisch muss einfach sein. Ich könnte jedenfalls nicht als Körnerfresser leben. Das ist doch unnormal, dass man kein Fleisch isst. Und wer halt politisch korrekt sein will, der kann ja sein Fleisch direkt beim Bio-Bauern oder im Bioladen kaufen.

PRO   **Margrit**, 18

Vegetarier essen viel mehr Obst und Gemüse, was für die Menschen viel gesünder ist. Und ich habe auch noch nie einen übergewichtigen Vegetarier gesehen. Ich weiß nicht genau, woran das liegt, aber vielleicht daran, dass Fleischprodukte viel mehr Fett enthalten als pflanzliche Produkte.

Tips for texts

➤ Look at how **aufhören** is used in the first sentence. Usually, when two verbs are used together, the second verb has **zu** before it. However, when the first verb is a *modal*, you don't need to use **zu**.

➤ **Dass** (in Janina's text) also sends the following verb to the end. It's used to *report* what someone says or thinks, and it signals that you have to look at the end of the clause for the verb that might unlock the meaning of the text.

➤ You can also *report* what people are saying without using **dass**, as Wiebke does: **Ich finde, Fleisch muss einfach sein**.

➤ To say 'more than', use **mehr als**.

➤ With 'who' tasks, there are often a lot of clues in the questions: they paraphrase the text, and so give you another chance to understand what's being said.

➤ In texts like this, which give a range of opinions, look for phrases that indicate how a person feels, such as **ich mag …**, **ich finde das total …**, **ich bin absolut gegen …**

"Vegetarisches Hundefutter" – Was?! Kein Fleisch??!!

7 Wer ist das? Schreib jeweils den richtigen Namen auf. (5 marks)

Beispiel:
  Sie findet es nicht normal, vegetarisch zu essen.   *Wiebke*

1 Sie isst kein Fleisch, aber sie isst Käse und Omeletts.   _____

2 Vegetarische Ernährung schmeckt ihr gar nicht.   _____

3 Sie kennt nur dünne Vegetarier.   _____

4 Sie findet vegetarische Ernährung gesünder als Fleisch.   _____

5 Sie empfiehlt Bioläden für Leute, die Mitleid mit Tieren haben. _____

Name/
Group:

Stark reduziert!
Diese Woche im Angebot!

Frische Erdbeerjogurts
0,50€ der Becher

Serbische Bohnensuppe
2€ die Dose

Fettarme Kartoffelchips
0,75€ die Tüte

Zarte Vollmilchschokolade
1,50€ die Tafel

Schwarzwälder Kirschtorte
5,00€ das Stück

1 You're shopping in Germany and you're checking the prices. Answer the questions. (4 marks)

Beispiel: What costs 5 euros a slice?

Black Forest gateau

1 What costs 2 euros a tin? _____

2 What is low in fat? _____

3 How much is milk chocolate? _____

4 What contains strawberries? _____

2 Schreib den richtigen Buchstaben in jedes Kästchen. (4 marks)

Beispiel: *Ein Kilo Käse bitte.* B

1 *Es tut mir Leid, aber ich habe keine Äpfel.*

2 *Entschuldigung … haben Sie zufällig Kekse?*

3 *Bitte schön, eine Tafel Schokolade. Sonst noch etwas?*

4 *Ein Kilo Hackfleisch. Das macht fünf Euro insgesamt.*

A
D
B
E
C
F

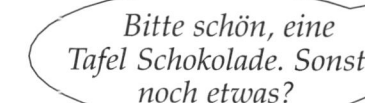

Clever clues

➤ In Ex 1, each of the food items is a *compound word* comprising two or more parts. If you know one part, you've got a good chance of working out the rest. Try covering half of each word and trying to recognize the other half!

➤ Look for *negatives*. In Ex 2, only one of the sentences is negative, so the corresponding picture should be easy to find!

➤ Ignore 'filler' words like **zufällig** (Ex 2 Qu 2), but make sure you don't overlook words that tell you *who* is talking. If someone says **sonst noch etwas** (Ex 2 Qu 3), for instance, is it the shop assistant or the customer?

Check the *Vital Vocabulary* (worksheet 50) if you need help with any of these words.

1 Schreib den richtigen Buchstaben in jedes Kästchen. (5 marks)

Beispiel: Diese Hose passt mir nicht! **C**

1 Dieser Pullover ist mir zu eng. ☐

2 Die Jacke gefällt mir gar nicht! Die Farbe ist ätzend! ☐

3 Die Schuhe sind mir leider zu teuer – fünfzig Euro kann ich mir nicht leisten. ☐

4 So ein Hemd würde ich **nie** tragen. Es ist altmodisch. ☐

5 Dieses Kleid ist mir zu groß. ☐

2 *Im Kaufhaus:* Wo kauft man folgende Sachen? Schreib **U**, **E**, **1**, **2** oder **3** in das Kästchen. (5 marks)

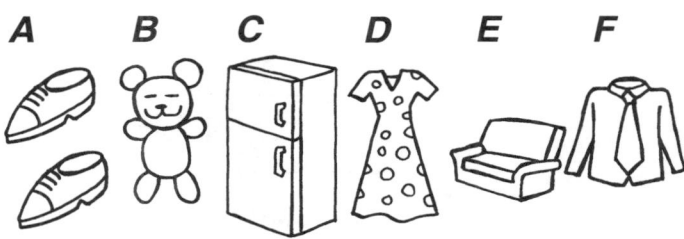

A   B   C   D   E   F

Beispiel:

2   ☐   ☐   ☐   ☐   ☐

3. STOCK	Möbel, Haushaltswaren
2. STOCK	Herrenmode, Schuhabteilung
1. STOCK	Kinderabteilung: Spielzeug usw.
ERDGESCHOSS	Parfüm, Damenmode, Schmuck
UNTERGESCHOSS	Elektrogeräte: Kühlschränke usw.

Clever clues

➤ There are lots of *adjectives* in Ex 1 – make sure you know them all!

➤ Look for *cognates*, as always. Lots of words here (like **Pullover**, **Jacke**, **Schuhe** in Ex 1) are from English – or (like **Möbel** in Ex 2) from French. Make sure you learn the words that *aren't* like the English, e.g. **Hemd** and **Kleid** (Ex 1).

➤ In the names of departments (Ex 2), there are lots of *compounds* again. Look for *key word parts* that give you a clue to what that department sells. For instance, if you see **Herren**, you know it's something to do with men.

Use the *Vital Vocabulary* (worksheet 50) again if you need to – and check this vocabulary against the notes you've made in the past.

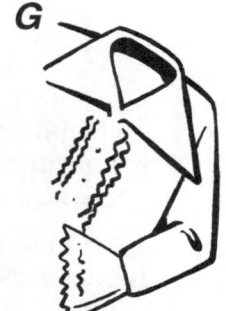

'Herrenmode', 'Damenmode', 'Kinderabteilung' ... but where's the dogs' department?!

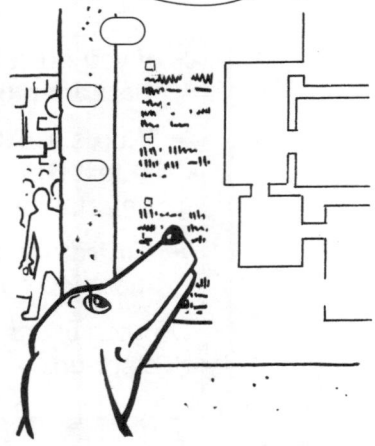

A **Riesige Oldtimer-Ausstellung!** Unter der Lupe: PKWs der 50er Jahre. Frankfurter Messe, 7. bis 9. Oktober. Eintritt 3€. Ticket-Hotline: 29 76 89 50

B

HALLENBAD
Biegenstraße,
35000 Marburg a. d. Lahn.
Kinderbecken.
Eintritt 2€. Ermäßigungen für
Familien. Öffnungszeiten 9-19
Uhr. Telefon: 65 93 45 28

C **Jazzabend. Das Genie von Bix Beiderbecke.** Im Hinkelkeller, Göttinger Straße 84, Gießen. Eintritt 6€ oder 4€ mit Studentenausweis. 8. Oktober ab 21 Uhr. Tel: 58 34 59 21

D **Große Haustierausstellung,** Dresdner Messe, 8. und 9. Oktober, 8 bis 22 Uhr (Samstag) und 9 bis 20 Uhr (Sonntag). Mehr als 1000 Aussteller und 5000 Tiere. Eintritt 5€. Tel: 63 19 52 39

E **Flohmarkt am Marktplatz,** Limburg a. d. Lahn, Sonntag 9. Oktober ab 10 Uhr. Mehr als 500 Verkäufer und Händler. Fernseher, Telefone usw. – alles aus Kunststoff. Eintritt gratis. Tel: 43 21 68 42

1 Was ist das? Schreib den richtigen Buchstaben in jedes Kästchen. (5 marks)

Beispiel: Dort gibt es viele Katzen. [D]

1 Dort sind mehr als 500 Leute, die alte Radios usw. verkaufen. ☐

2 Für drei Euro kann man alte Autos sehen. ☐

3 Es würde Leute interessieren, die gern altmodische Musik hören. ☐

4 In diesem Gebäude kann man schwimmen gehen. ☐

5 Dorthin kann man gehen ohne zu zahlen. ☐

A flea market?! Think I'll steer clear of that! But there might be some cats worth chasing at the pet show.

👉 Handy hints

➤ If you don't know **Oldtimer** (text A), **PKW** should help. It stands for **Personenkraftwagen** – can you think of another word for that?

➤ Words like **Ausstellung**, which appear with others (**Oldtimer-** in text A, **Haustier-** in text D), give a clue to the meaning of the word they're linked with. What kind of entertainment are these?

➤ **Eintritt** (text B) is from **treten** ('to step, tread') and **ein** ('in'). Can you work out the meaning here? It's usually followed by a price in euros.

Do your usual *Vital Vocabulary* check (worksheet 50) if there's anything you still need to clear up.

Name/
Group:

Wie wichtig ist Mode für dich?

Wir haben mit Jella (17), Carla (16) und Arno (17) gesprochen um herauszufinden, wie wichtig Mode für sie ist.

Carla: Für mich ist Mode nicht so wichtig. Ich schaue mir zwar manchmal auch Modezeitschriften an, aber meistens stehen mir die Sachen, die die Models in den Magazinen tragen, sowieso nicht. Deshalb trage ich oft total alte Sachen. Ich finde das sehr praktisch, da brauche ich nicht so viel Geld für Klamotten auszugeben.

Arno: Mir ist es eigentlich völlig egal, wie ich aussehe. Für mich ist einfach nur wichtig, dass die Sachen, die ich trage, mich vor Kälte oder Regen schützen und dass ich mich in ihnen absolut wohl fühle. Was mich an der Mode absolut nervt, ist, dass zwar alle Leute individuell und toll aussehen wollen, aber dann alle dieselbe Uniform tragen, nämlich die neue Frühjahrsmode. Alle haben dieselben Farben an und denselben Stil.

Jella: Mir macht Mode sehr viel Spaß. Ich versuche immer herauszufinden, was der neueste Trend ist. Und dann trage ich die Sachen, noch bevor sie irgendjemand anders in der Schule anhat. Oft kommen dann andere Mädchen zu mir und sagen „Wow, wo hast du den Rock her, der sieht ja klasse aus!" Das gibt mir dann immer ein gutes Gefühl.

1 Wer ist das? Schreib jeweils den richtigen Namen auf. (5 marks)

Beispiel: Wer interessiert sich gar nicht

für Mode? *Arno*

1 Wer muss immer als Erste die neuesten

Moden kaufen? _____

2 Wer trägt meistens alte Kleidung? _____

3 Wer mag die Moden meistens nicht, die

die Models anhaben? _____

4 Wer will einfach warme und bequeme

Kleidung haben? _____

5 Wer liest ab und zu Modezeitschriften?

_____

Tips for texts

➤ There are some quite complex sentences in this text, especially those with *relative pronouns*. Can you work out what Carla's **die Sachen, die die Models ...** means (5 words, 3 of which are **die**!)?

➤ **Zwar** and **nämlich** are often used as 'sentence-fillers' – they aren't crucial to the meaning. Can you work out what they mean, though?

➤ Look out for *reported speech*, both with and without **dass**. Only when **dass** is used does the verb in the subordinate clause go to the end.

➤ With 'who' tasks, there are often a lot of clues in the questions: they paraphrase the text and so give you another chance to understand it.

➤ The German for 'I don't care' uses an *impersonal* construction: 'it's all the same to me'. Can you find the exact phrase?

➤ 'I must' can be expressed in two ways. One is **ich muss** – can you find the other?

➤ Look for words and phrases that give clues to people's *opinions*. **Nervt mich** and **macht mir Spaß** are two examples – can you work out their meanings and find others?

➤ **Bevor** is similar to its English equivalent, so the meaning is easy to guess. Don't forget its effect on word order, though.

Home, health and fitness

◆ Foundation and ◆◆ Foundation/Higher (WS 42–44)

Nouns

Masculine
der (Apfel)saft	(apple) juice
der Käse	cheese
der Nachtisch	dessert
der Schinken	ham
der Supermarkt	supermarket

Feminine
die (Erdbeer)konfitüre	(strawberry) jam
die Hauptspeise	main course

Neuter
das Brötchen	bread roll
das Fleisch	meat
das Gemüse	vegetable(s)
das Müsli	muesli
das Obst	fruit

Plural
die Eier	eggs

> *Try learning vocabulary in pairs or opposites, e.g. 'Schinken/Eier'.*

Verbs and useful expressions

ab und zu	now and then
abends	in the evenings
abspülen	to wash up
am Wochenende	at the weekend
das Bett machen	to make the bed
dauern	to last
einkaufen	to go shopping
gesund	healthy, healthily
sich hinsetzen	to sit down
jeden Morgen	every morning
sich konzentrieren (auf)	to concentrate (on)
normalerweise	normally
den Rasen mähen	to mow the lawn
Spaß machen	to be fun, be enjoyable
Staub saugen	to vacuum
teurer	dearer, more expensive
den Tisch decken	to lay the table

Work and shopping

◆ Foundation and ◆◆ Foundation/Higher (WS 46–48)

Nouns

Masculine
der Aussteller	exhibitor
der Becher	pot
der Eintritt	entrance (fee)
der Flohmarkt	flea market
der Händler	dealer
der Kunststoff	plastic
der Oldtimer	classic car
der PKW	(private) car
der Schmuck	jewellery
der Studentenausweis	student ID card
der Verkäufer	seller, vendor

Feminine
die Ausstellung	exhibition
die (Bohnen)suppe	(bean) soup
die Damenmode	women's fashion
die Ermäßigung	reduction
die 50er Jahre	the 50s
die Herrenmode	men's fashion
die Hose	trousers
die (Kinder)abteilung	children's department
die Öffnungszeit	opening time
die Schuhabteilung	shoe department
die Schwarzwälder Kirschtorte	Black Forest gateau
die Tafel	bar (of chocolate)
die Tüte	bag
die (Vollmilch)schokolade	(milk) chocolate

Neuter
das Erdgeschoss	ground floor
das Hallenbad	indoor pool
das Hemd	shirt
das Kaufhaus	department store
das Kinderbecken	children's pool
das Möbel	(piece of) furniture
das Spielzeug	toy(s)
das Stück	piece, slice; item
das Untergeschoss	basement

Plural
die Elektrogeräte	electrical appliances
die Haushaltswaren	household goods
die Kartoffelchips	potato crisps
die Kekse	biscuits

> *If you organize the words into groups you can make other (possibly silly!) words out of their initial letters, to help you remember them. This is called a 'mnemonic'. For instance, you can make HEKK with the plural nouns – but don't forget what each letter stands for!*

Verbs and useful expressions

altmodisch	old-fashioned
im Angebot	on offer
dieser/diese/dieses	this
eng	tight, narrow
fettarm	low-fat
gratis	free (of charge)
sich (dat.) leisten	to afford
unter der Lupe	a closer look at, in depth
reduziert	reduced
würde(n)	would
zart	mild, tender

Name/
Group:

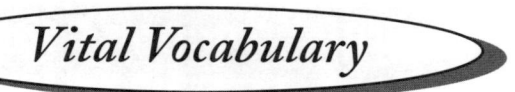
Vital Vocabulary

Home, health and fitness
◆ ◆ ◆ Higher (WS 45)

Nouns

Masculine
der Bio-Bauer	*organic farmer*
der Bioladen	*wholefood shop*
der Körnerfresser	*'lentil-eater', 'tofu-botherer'*
der Mensch	*human being(s), man*
der Vegetarier	*vegetarian*

Feminine
die Ernährung	*food, nourishment*
die Idee	*idea*

Neuter
das Fett	*fat, oil*
das Fleisch	*meat*
das Mitleid	*sympathy, pity*

Verbs and useful expressions

absolut gar nichts	*absolutely nothing at all*
aufhören	*to stop*
enthalten	*to contain*
gesünder	*healthier*
halten von	*to think (have an opinion) of*
in der heutigen Zeit	*nowadays*
jedenfalls	*in any case*
neulich	*recently*
pflanzlich	*plant-based*
politisch korrekt	*politically correct*
probieren	*to try*
scheußlich	*awful, horrible*
schmecken (nach)	*to taste (of)*
das schmeckt mir	*I like (the taste of) it*
töten	*to kill*
übergewichtig	*overweight*
unnormal	*not normal*
verrückt	*mad*
woran das liegt	*why that is*

Another way to learn words is to list them with the vowels missing and then try to fill in the vowels, and the meanings, from memory. It's harder than you think!

Work and shopping
◆ ◆ ◆ Higher (WS 49)

Remember to say the words out loud when learning vocabulary, to practise your pronunciation.

Nouns

Masculine
der Regen	*rain*
der Stil	*style*
der Trend	*trend*

Feminine
die Frühjahrsmode	*spring fashion*
die Kälte	*cold*
die Mode	*fashion*
die Modezeitschrift	*fashion magazine*

Neuter
das Gefühl	*feeling*

Verbs and useful expressions

anhaben	*to have on, wear*
sich (dat.) anschauen	*to look at*
ausgeben	*to spend*
aussehen	*to look, appear*
der/die/dasselbe	*the same*
mir ist es egal	*I don't care*
individuell	*individual(ly)*
irgendjemand anders	*anyone else*
klasse	*great!*
manchmal	*sometimes*
nämlich	*that is, namely*
nerven	*to get on (someone's) nerves*
noch bevor	*even before*
praktisch	*practical*
schützen	*to protect*
stehen (es steht mir)	*to fit, look good on, suit*
wichtig	*important*
sich wohl fühlen	*to feel well*
zwar (… aber)	*it's true that (… but)*

1 Look at the sentences about appointments and the people in the pictures. Who's waiting in the right place at the right time – and who isn't? Put a tick or a cross in the box on the picture. (5 marks)

Beispiel: Wir treffen uns um acht Uhr neben dem Bahnhof.
1 Ich warte auf dich um halb neun vor der Kirche.
2 Wir treffen uns um zehn Uhr hinter dem Supermarkt.
3 Wir sehen uns um halb zehn in der Disko.
4 Wir treffen uns um neun Uhr neben der Schule.
5 Ich warte auf dich um elf Uhr vor dem Einkaufszentrum.

> I think I've been stood up. She said 'um halb acht vor der Kirche'. Well, this is the church and it's half eight on the dot – so where is she?

> Argh! I've just remembered: 'halb acht' means half seven! This is going to take some explaining ...

Clever clues

➤ Lots of *times* here. You surely know by now about 'half past' and 'half to' (although our friend doesn't!). *Don't forget:* **halb acht** = 'half *to* eight' = 'half past seven'!

➤ Do you know your *prepositions*? If you've arranged to meet someone in front of the church, you don't want to be waiting behind it! Here are the most important ones: **vor** 'in front of', **hinter** 'behind', **neben** 'next to'.

➤ What about your *reflexive verbs*? **Sich treffen** and **sich sehen** don't mean 'we meet ourselves' and 'we see ourselves' – so what *do* they mean?

➤ How are you on places in town? The ones used here are relatively easy – but there's a long list of them to remember ...

... so see the *Vital Vocabulary* (worksheet 62) if your memory needs jogging!

Name/
Group:

Tobias

Ich spiele gern Fußball, aber ich kann Tennis nicht leiden.

Lukas **Laura**

Ich lese und sehe gern fern, aber Musikhören kann ich nicht leiden.

Ich spiele sehr gern am Computer, aber ich treibe nicht gern Sport.

Lena

Ich gehe gern schwimmen, aber ich hasse Fußball.

Ich spiele sehr gern Handball, aber Skifahren kann ich nicht leiden.

Katharina

1 *Freizeit!* Schreib jeweils den richtigen Namen auf. Wer …
(5 marks)

1 … treibt nicht gern Sport? _____

2 … fährt nicht gern Ski? _____

3 … liest gern? _____

4 … kann Fußball nicht leiden? _____

5 … spielt nicht gern Tennis? _____

Clever clues

➤ **Gern** is a really important word. It's how to say you *like* doing something, but in German it comes *after* what you like doing.

➤ These texts use two different ways of saying you *hate* things: can you work out what they are?

➤ Don't forget how to say 'do sport' in German: it's **Sport treiben**.

And don't forget the *Vital Vocabulary* (worksheet 62) if you've forgotten any of these words!

Mit vier Füßen kann ich Fußball gut spielen …

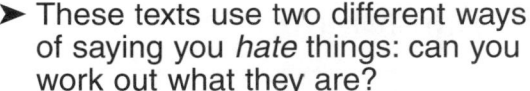

… aber Handball kann ich nicht!

Ultimate Frisbee braucht Ultimate Spieler!

Ultimate Frisbee

Das Spiel kommt aus Amerika. Dort spielen High-School-Kids seit 1968 Ultimate Frisbee. Heute spielt man es in vierundzwanzig Ländern und jedes Jahr gibt es die Ultimate Frisbee-World Games. Beim Ultimate Frisbee spielt man auf einem großen Feld plus zwei Endzonen. Es gibt zwei Teams. Ein Team muss die Frisbeescheibe in die Endzone des anderen Teams werfen. Wenn ein Spieler die Frisbee hat, bleibt er stehen und wirft die Frisbee einem anderen Spieler zu.

Es gibt keine Spielzeit. Das Spiel ist zu Ende, wenn ein Team genug Punkte hat. Beim Ultimate Frisbee gibt es auch keinen Schiedsrichter. Die Teams müssen das Spiel und die Regeln respektieren.

1 Schreib **R** (richtig), **F** (falsch) oder **?** (nicht im Text). (5 marks)

Beispiel:

In den USA spielt man seit den sechziger Jahren Ultimate Frisbee. `R`

1 Man spielt es heute in 42 Ländern. ☐

2 Die Mannschaften tragen gelbe Hemden. ☐

3 Das Spiel dauert zwei Stunden. ☐

4 Bei einem Ultimate-Frisbee-Spiel gibt es zwei Mannschaften. ☐

5 Der Schiedsrichter steht am Rande des Felds. ☐

 Handy hints

> ➤ Look for the **key words** in each sentence of this text. You won't understand all of it – but you don't need to! The important words are **Amerika, 1968, in vierundzwanzig Ländern, jedes Jahr, Ultimate Frisbee-World Games** … Can you carry on?

> ➤ Some words have difficult plurals! **Ländern** (Qu 1) is one of these. To find the singular, take the **-n** off the end (it's in the dative here) and then take away the plural markers, which are the **Umlaut** and the **-er** ending. What are you left with?

> ➤ Don't forget that after **wenn** the word order changes. The sentence beginning **Wenn ein Spieler die Frisbee hat, …** is quite complicated. Try to work out what it means:

• **Stehen bleiben** is an expression made up of two verbs (**stehen** and **bleiben**). What does **bleibt er stehen** mean in this text?

• **Zuwerfen** is not only a separable verb, it also has *two* objects. Can you (a) find the objects in the text and (b) work out what the verb means?

As usual, the *Vital Vocabulary* (worksheet 62) is there if you need any help.

Name/ Group:

❈ ❈ ❈ Eislaufen ❈ ❈ ❈ ❈

Eislaufen oder Schlittschuhlaufen ist ein toller Winterspaß. Bei großer Kälte kann man auf Seen oder Flüssen Schlittschuh laufen. Natürlich kann man auch zu den anderen Jahreszeiten Schlittschuh laufen – in einer Halle. Aber draußen auf dem Eis zu laufen ist etwas ganz Besonderes.

Dieses Hobby gibt es seit fast achthundert Jahren in Europa. Die ersten Schlittschuhe mit Metall-Kufe kamen aus Holland. Man benutzt sie dort seit etwa 1250 um im Winter schneller von einem Ort zum anderen zu kommen. Von Holland aus kam das Schlittschuhlaufen nach England. 1784 wurde der erste Schlittschuhverein in Edinburgh gegründet und 1867 der „Wiener Eislaufverein" in Österreich. Dieser Verein organisierte 1882 das erste internationale Eislauftreffen.

Die ersten Weltmeisterschaften fanden 1896 in St. Petersburg statt. Diese Weltmeisterschaften waren nur für Herren. Aber schon 1906 gab es Weltmeisterschaften für Herren, Damen und Paare. Die ersten dreifachen Sprünge beim Kürlaufen konnte man 1962 bei den Weltmeisterschaften in Prag sehen.

❈ ❈ ❈ ❈ ❈ ❈ ❈ ❈ ❈ ❈ ❈

Tips for texts

➤ There are a few **verbal nouns** in this text, and two of them tell you what the subject matter is. If you can't find them, they also occur in the questions. What are they?

➤ To find out where skates come from, look for a **country name** – and make sure you pick the right one!

➤ There are quite a few **dates** in the text, so the questions containing these should be fairly easy. But make sure you associate each date with the right fact: look for the **key words** that go with each.

➤ The words for 'club' and 'meeting' will be useful. The word for 'meeting' is just the infinitive of the verb meaning 'to meet'. What is it?

➤ As usual, look for **compound words**. To work out what took place in Prague in 1962, you need to be able to break down **Weltmeisterschaften**. The last part (-**schaften**) is a suffix meaning '-ness' or '-ship'. The other two words are reasonably guessable – can you work out what they mean?

➤ It's easy to confuse the words **ein paar** and **ein Paar**! One means 'a few' and the other means 'a couple' or 'a pair' – which one is used here?

If you need vocabulary help, turn quickly to the *Vital Vocabulary* (worksheet 63)!

---

1 Read the article about ice-skating and answer the questions in English. (7 marks)

Beispiel: How long has skating as a hobby existed in Europe? <u>*800 years*</u>

1 Where did the first ice-skates come from?

2 What were they used for in the beginning? _____

3 When was the first skating club in Edinburgh founded? _____

4 Which club organized the first international meeting? _____

5 Who were the first world championships for? _____

6 When did championships for women, men and pairs begin? _____

7 In what event in Prague in 1962 did the first triple jump feature? _____

Ich esse viele Äpfel, aber auch viel Kuchen!

Schokolade schmeckt mir sehr, aber ab und zu esse ich einige Trauben.

Ich esse zu viele Pommes frites, aber zum Frühstück esse ich ein Ei.

Ich esse jeden Tag einen Salat, aber ich esse auch viele Bonbons.

Mein Lieblingsessen ist Pasta, aber ich esse auch gern Kartoffelchips!

1 Gesund oder ungesund? Mach zwei Listen auf Englisch.

Ich esse oft Hähnchen, aber manchmal kaufe ich mir einen Hamburger.

GESUND ✔ **UNGESUND ✗**

Beispiel: apples   cakes

_____ _____ (2 marks)

_____ _____ (2 marks)

_____ _____ (2 marks)

_____ _____ (2 marks)

_____ _____ (2 marks)

2 You see this poster offering part-time jobs on the wall in a German school. What jobs can you do on the following days? (5 marks)

Beispiel: Sunday   *Feeding animals*

1 Friday   _____

2 Wednesday   _____

3 Saturday   _____

4 Tuesday   _____

5 Thursday   _____

Brauchst du mehr Taschengeld?

Hier sind Jobs für alle!
Ruf an, wenn du einen Job möchtest!

Montag	Babysitten	0874 56732
Dienstag	Autowaschen	0931 94732
Mittwoch	Zeitungen austragen	0290 71536
Donnerstag	Kellner(in)	0356 79125
Freitag	Gartenarbeit	0582 39714
Samstag	Im Supermarkt arbeiten	0493 62014
Sonntag	Tiere füttern	0187 96032

Name/
Group:

1 *Das liebe Geld* – zwei Interviews

Erika (16) aus Erding

Ich bekomme 20 Euro Taschengeld, aber meine Eltern geben mir immer noch Geld dazu, wenn ich etwas Großes wie Klamotten oder Schulsachen brauche. Aber mit den 20 Euro komme ich nicht aus. Ich gehe einmal mit meiner Freundin abends ins Kino und schon sind sie weg.

Ich habe auch einen Nebenjob. Ich helfe mittwochabends einer alten Frau beim Einkaufen und mache ihre Wohnung sauber. Sie ist immer sehr großzügig und gibt mir pro Abend zehn bis fünfzehn Euro. Aber auch das Geld habe ich meistens am nächsten Tag schon wieder ausgegeben. Ich muss mir oft Geld von meinen Freundinnen leihen.

Birgit (17) aus Göppingen

Ich bekomme 25 Euro Taschengeld im Monat. Am Wochenende gehe ich immer in den Club. Das kostet natürlich viel Geld. Da bleibt für Klamotten, CDs oder Kosmetika nichts übrig. Deshalb habe ich einen Nebenjob. Ich arbeite samstagvormittags in einem Supermarkt. Der Job ist okay und dadurch habe ich genug Geld um mir die Sachen zu kaufen, die ich haben möchte. Mein Geld reicht gerade aus. Am Monatsende ist mein Portemonnaie meistens leer, aber dann ist ja zum Glück wieder Zahltag.

1 Wer geht wie mit Geld um? Schreib „Birgit" oder „Erika" auf. (5 marks)

Beispiel: Sie braucht viel Geld für Kleidung, Musik usw.   *Birgit*

1 Man gibt ihr noch etwas Geld um Kleidung usw. zu kaufen. _____

2 Am Wochenende hat sie einen Nebenjob. _____

3 Sie bekommt 10–15 Euro pro Woche von einer alten Dame. _____

4 Im Großen und Ganzen reicht ihr Geld. _____

5 Sie hat nie Geld genug. _____

2 SANDBOARDEN

Kennt ihr den „Monte Kaolino"? Das ist ein 120 Meter hoher Sandberg in der Oberpfalz (Bayern).

Jedes Jahr im Sommer trifft sich hier die internationale Snowboard-Elite. Denn dann finden auf dem „Monte Kaolino" die ‚Sandboarding-World-Championships' statt. Früher kamen zu den „Sandboarding-World-Championships" nur ein paar Snowboard-Profis, die nicht auf den Winter warten wollten. Heute ist die Weltmeisterschaft ein großes Festival mit Party-Programm für 20 000 Besucher.

Die Profi-Boarderinnen und -Boarder sind aber immer noch dabei. Denn es ist ein Abenteuer, auf dem Sandberg zu fahren. Die Piste ist 215 Meter lang und steiler als jede Schneepiste (50 Prozent) und es ist gefährlicher hier zu boarden als im Schnee. Wenn man im Sand fällt, rutscht man viele Meter, und das tut sehr weh. Aber auch wenn die meisten Profis nicht hinfallen, Sand bekommen hier alle Fahrerinnen und Fahrer in den Mund.

2 Schreib **R** (richtig), **F** (falsch) oder **?** (nicht im Text). (5 marks)

Beispiel:
Monte Kaolino ist ein 120 Meter hoher Sandberg.   R

1 Jedes Jahr im Winter treffen sich am Monte Kaolino die wichtigsten Leute der Snowboard-Welt. ☐

2 Bei den Sandboard-Weltmeisterschaften erwartet man heute 20 000 Besucher. ☐

3 Für die meisten Snowboarder ist Sandboarden leicht und etwas langweilig. ☐

4 Wenn man beim Sandboarden hinfällt, verletzt man sich leicht. ☐

5 Wenn man im Sand rutscht, verliert man oft das Sandboard. ☐

1 *Popularity poll:* here are your friend Silke's answers. Answer the questions. (5 marks)

A Meine Mutter ist nett und freundlich.

B Mein Hund, Tricksi, ist faul und etwas doof.

C Herr Schröder ist ungeduldig und sehr gemein.

D Frau Lüdecke ist fleißig, aber ziemlich langweilig.

E Otto ist hilfsbereit und sehr interessant.

F Anke ist hässlich und etwas dick.

Beispiel:
Who is rather boring? _Frau Lüdecke_

1 Who is impatient? _____

2 Who is lazy? _____

3 Who is ugly? _____

4 Who is interesting? _____

5 Who is friendly? _____

I know Dick is short for Richard, but what's Doof short for?

'Dick' is fat in German and 'doof' is stupid!

Clever clues

➤ In these sentences there are several adjectives describing people's ***personality*** and other characteristics.

• If an adjective in German begins with a negative prefix like **un-**, it probably begins in English with 'in-', 'im-' or 'un-', which are negative prefixes in English. So **ungeduldig** (C) is 'in-' or 'im-' something, which may help you a bit.

• Look for ***clues*** to the meaning of the adjectives by breaking them up. If you know **Hilfe**, you're half way to **hilfsbereit** (E) – but what about **hässlich** and **dick** (F)?

Don't forget to look up any adjectives you've forgotten in the *Vital Vocabulary* (worksheet 62).

Name/
Group:

> neu! **OSTENDER**

Die neue Seifenoper im deutschen Fernsehen!
Laura kommt sehr gut mit Jonas aus.
Jonas findet Alexander sehr nett.
Alexander findet Laura sehr doof.
Katharina findet Laura sehr sympathisch.
Jonas geht Sophie auf die Nerven.

It says Laura is 'sympathisch'. But why does she feel sorry for the others?

'Sympathisch' doesn't mean sympathetic in German!

1 Schreib **R** (richtig), **F** (falsch) oder **?** (nicht im Text). (5 marks)

Beispiel:
Alexander kommt gut mit Jonas aus.   [R]

1 Laura findet Jonas sympathisch. ☐

2 Katharina mag Laura nicht. ☐

3 Sophie ist eine Freundin von Alexander. ☐

4 Sophie mag Jonas nicht. ☐

5 Alexander ist Lauras bester Freund. ☐

2 Read the text again. Who … (5 marks)

Beispiel:
… likes Laura?   *Katharina*

1 … thinks Alexander is nice? _____

2 … gets on Sophie's nerves? _____

3 … doesn't like Jonas? _____

4 … thinks Laura is stupid? _____

5 … gets on well with Jonas? _____

Clever clues

➤ The verb **auskommen** is separable. It has nothing to do with coming out! See if you can work out what it means and how to use it in a sentence.

➤ Some adjectives are *false friends*. **Sympathisch** doesn't mean what you would expect it to!

➤ What do you think **auf die Nerven gehen** means? (The English phrase has 'nerves' in it as well.)

Don't forget that the *Vital Vocabulary* (worksheet 62) can help you fill any gaps in your knowledge.

Name/
Group:

„*Liebe Tante Julia ...*"

Meine Mutter geht mir total auf die Nerven! Sie meckert die ganze Zeit und verlangt, dass ich immer bis 11 Uhr zu Hause bin. Hilf mir – bitte!
Jörg, 16

Meine Freundin hat einen kleinen Hund, und er bellt und springt ständig in die Luft. Das nervt mich sehr, aber was kann ich tun? Ich will meine Freundin nicht verärgern.
Lutz, 19

Meine kleine Schwester nervt mich. Ich muss mein Zimmer mit ihr teilen, aber sie redet immer mit mir, wenn ich meine Hausaufgaben mache oder einschlafen will. HILFE!!
Wiebke, 18

Meine Mutter erlaubt mir nicht mit meinem Freund zu telefonieren. Ich habe mein eigenes Handy, aber ihrer Meinung nach rede ich zu lange mit ihm. Das finde ich unfair! Hilfe!
Gabi, 17

1 Lies die Texte. Wer ... (5 marks)

Beispiel: ... hasst das Haustier seiner Freundin?   *Lutz*

1 ... darf ihren Freund nicht anrufen?   _____

2 ... kann nicht schlafen, weil jemand sie stört?   _____

3 ... darf nicht zu spät nach Hause kommen?   _____

4 ... hat kein eigenes Schlafzimmer?   _____

5 ... möchte seine Freundin nicht böse machen?   _____

Gabi's got a 'Handy'. Yes, but a handy what?!

👉 Handy hints

➤ **Auf die Nerven gehen** (Jörg) is a way of saying someone gets on someone's nerves. Can you find another way in these texts of saying the same thing?

➤ **Bis** (Jörg) can mean 'until'. However, here it means something else. What?

➤ **Ihrer** (or **meiner**) **Meinung nach** (Gabi) is a useful phrase, because it means you don't have to use a separate clause to report what someone said. What does it mean?

➤ What can you say about the meaning of **dürfen** (Qus 1 & 3) and **(jemandem) erlauben** (Gabi)? This is an example of the questions *paraphrasing* a word or words in the text (i.e. saying the same thing in a different way).

A 'Handy' is a mobile phone in German!

Name/
Group:

Urlaubs*flirt*

1 SCHUSS: *Irma, hattest du schon einmal einen Urlaubsflirt?*

IRMA: Ja, letztes Jahr. Da war ich mit meinen Eltern auf Sardinien, in Italien. Meine Eltern sind nicht sehr aktiv und deshalb war es am Anfang nicht sehr spannend. Aber wir haben in einem großen Hotel gewohnt und dort habe ich dann viele nette Jugendliche getroffen. Mit dieser Clique bin ich immer an den Strand gegangen und dort habe ich Francesco kennen gelernt. Seine Eltern haben dort eine Bar. Er war mit seiner Clique auch immer am Strand.

SCHUSS: *Hast du heute noch Kontakt zu Francesco?*

IRMA: Nein, es war klar, dass das nur ein Urlaubsflirt war. Wir hatten viel Spaß zusammen und mein Urlaub war dadurch lustig.

2 SCHUSS: *Elias, hattest du schon einmal einen Urlaubsflirt?*

ELIAS: Ja, vor zwei Jahren. Da habe ich mit meinem Fahrradverein unseren Partnerverein in Frankreich besucht und mit einem Mädchen aus dem Verein hatte ich einen Urlaubsflirt. Camille war freundlich und intelligent.

SCHUSS: *Bist du richtig mit ihr gegangen?*

ELIAS: Nein, nicht richtig. Ihr Freund war auch in dem Verein und natürlich bei allen Unternehmungen mit dabei.

SCHUSS: *Hast du heute noch Kontakt zu ihr?*

ELIAS: Nein, aber ihr Verein kommt uns in diesem Herbst besuchen und wer weiß? Vielleicht ist sie ja nicht mehr mit ihrem Freund zusammen … Für mich ist sie immer noch ein Traumgirl.

2 Lies jetzt den Text über Elias und schreib **R** (richtig), **F** (falsch) oder **?** (nicht im Text). (4 marks)

Beispiel:
Elias hatte einen Urlaubsflirt mit einem Mädchen aus Frankreich. [R]

1 Camille besuchte Elias' Fahrradverein in Deutschland. ☐

2 Camille hatte schon einen Freund, aber das war kein Problem. ☐

3 Elias und Camille sind schwimmen gegangen. ☐

4 Elias hofft Camille nochmal zu sehen. ☐

1 Lies den Text über Irma und wähl entweder A, B, C oder D. (4 marks)

Beispiel: Am Anfang hat Irma die Ferien ziemlich **A** langweilig **B** interessant **C** anstrengend **D** aufregend gefunden. [A]

1 Sie war mit **A** Freunden **B** Verwandten **C** Schulkameraden **D** Kollegen dort. ☐

2 Im Hotel hat sie **A** nur mit ihren Eltern geredet **B** mit niemandem gesprochen **C** viele Leute kennen gelernt **D** nur ferngesehen. ☐

3 Francesco hatte **A** viele Verwandte **B** nur ein paar Freunde **C** einige Freunde, die nicht sehr freundlich waren **D** viele Freunde, die oft dabei waren. ☐

4 Mit Francesco hat Irma **A** viel Spaß **B** viel Mühe **C** viel zu tun **D** viel Pech gehabt. ☐

They never take <u>me</u> on holiday with them, so what chance have I got of a holiday romance?

Tips for texts

➤ Look for the usual *word-order clues*: information will always be in the order 'when–how–where (to)', and that can be very helpful in working out the meaning of a sentence.

➤ Try to understand the *gist* of the texts. If you don't know **Clique** (text 1) you can probably work out what it means, because Irma says **viele nette Jugendliche**, and then refers to them immediately afterwards as **diese(r) Clique**. Taken together, this makes the meaning pretty clear.

➤ Look for help in the *questions*. With multiple-choice questions, it's usually easy to eliminate one or two of the options – which gives you a 50% chance of a correct answer.

Name/
Group:

Vital Vocabulary

Try making puzzles for yourself (or your friends!) using the words you want to remember. You could do anagrams, crosswords, disguised letters, definitions ... it all makes it a bit more fun than just learning lists by heart – and it helps you learn them better as well!

Leisure

◆ Foundation and ◆ ◆ Foundation/Higher (WS 52–54)

Nouns

Masculine
der Bahnhof	*station*
der Fußball	*football*
der Schiedsrichter	*referee*

Feminine
die Disko	*disco*
die Frisbee(scheibe)	*frisbee (disk)*
die Kirche	*church*
die Mannschaft	*team*
die Schule	*school*

Neuter
das Einkaufszentrum	*shopping centre*
das Feld	*field, pitch*
das Land (Länder)	*country; region of a country*
das Skifahren	*skiing*
das Spiel	*game*

Verbs and useful expressions
fernsehen	*to watch TV*
hassen	*to hate*
hinter	*behind*
jedes Jahr	*every year*
(etwas/jemanden) nicht leiden können	*not to be able to stand (something/someone)*
lesen	*to read*
Musik hören	*to listen to music*
neben	*next to*
nochmal	*again*
schwimmen gehen	*to go swimming*
wir sehen uns (sich sehen)	*we'll see each other (followed by a date, place or time)*
Sport treiben	*to do sport*
stehen bleiben	*to keep still, stand still*
wir treffen uns (sich treffen)	*we'll meet (followed by a date, place or time)*
vor	*in front of*
warten auf	*to wait for*
zuwerfen (er wirft ... zu)	*to throw at*

Character and relationships

◆ Foundation and ◆ ◆ Foundation/Higher (WS 58–60)

See how many words you can memorize in a fixed time. Then try to do more words in less time ...

Verbs and useful expressions
auskommen mit	*to get on with*
bellen	*to bark*
bis 11 Uhr	*by 11 o'clock*
dick	*fat*
doof	*stupid*
echt	*real(ly)*
einschlafen	*to go to sleep*
erlauben (+ dat.)	*to allow*
etwas	*somewhat, rather; something*
faul	*lazy*
fleißig	*hard-working*
freundlich	*friendly*
(sie) geht mir auf die Nerven	*(she) gets on my nerves*
gemein	*mean*
hässlich	*ugly*
hilfsbereit	*helpful*
interessant	*interesting*
ich kann.(ihn) nicht leiden	*I can't stand (him)*
meckern	*to nag, 'get at'; to bicker*
ihrer Meinung nach	*in her opinion*
nerven	*to get on someone's nerves*
nett	*nice*
reden mit	*to speak/talk to*
springen	*to jump*
ständig	*all the time*
sympathisch	*nice, kind*
teilen	*to share*
ich telefoniere mit meiner Mutter	*I'm phoning my mother*
ungeduldig	*impatient*
verärgern	*to annoy, upset*
verlangen	*to demand*
versuchen	*to try*
ziemlich	*quite*

Name/
Group:

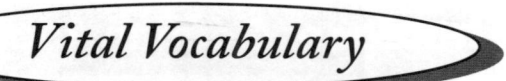
Leisure

◆ ◆ ◆ **Higher (WS 55)**

Nouns

Masculine
der Ort	*place*
der Sprung	*jump*
der Verein	*club*
der Winterspaß	*winter fun*

Feminine
die Jahreszeit	*season*
die Kufe	*runner*
die Weltmeisterschaft	*world championship*

Neuter
das Eislaufen	*ice-skating, speed-skating*
das Kürlaufen	*free-skating*
das Paar	*couple, pair*
das Schlittschuhlaufen	*ice-skating*
das Treffen	*meeting*

Verbs and useful expressions

dreifach	*triple*
Eis laufen/Schlittschuh laufen	*to ice-skate, speed skate*
etwa	*about*
etwas ganz Besonderes	*something quite special*
gründen	*to found*
stattfinden	*to take place*
Wiener	*Viennese*

Carry your list of words around with you, and get it out whenever you can to revise the words. You might get odd looks from people on the bus – but you'll do well in your exam!

Character and relationships

◆ ◆ ◆ **Higher (WS 61)**

Nouns

Masculine
der (Fahrrad)verein	*(cycling) club*
der/die Jugendliche	*young person*
der Spaß	*fun*
der Strand	*beach*
der Urlaubsflirt	*holiday romance*

Feminine
die Clique	*group of friends*
die Unternehmung	*activity, venture*

Verbs and useful expressions

kennen lernen	*to get to know*
lustig	*fun*
richtig mit jemandem gehen	*to go out with someone properly*
spannend	*exciting*
sympathisch	*nice, kind*
treffen	*to meet*
verschieden	*different*
zusammen	*together*

Try keying in vocabulary on a computer, with the English. Delete the English, and then go back to it later. Can you put the English back in? Then do it the other way round, which is harder!

Name/ Group:	© Mary Glasgow Magazines 2003	63

1 Bist du ein Umweltfreund? Schreib den richtigen Buchstaben in jedes Kästchen. (5 marks)

Beispiel: | Benutzen Sie Mehrwegflaschen! | B

1 | Bringen Sie Ihr Altpapier zum Recyclingcontainer! | ☐

2 | Kaufen Sie Obst der Saison! | ☐

3 | Nicht baden – beim Duschen Wasser sparen! | ☐

4 | Benutzen Sie Energiesparbirnen! | ☐

5 | Lassen Sie Ihren Computer nicht auf „Stand-by"! | ☐

BIRNEN
ENERGIESPARBIRNEN
6 €

> What kind of pears are energy-saving pears? I don't get it ...

A | B | C

D | E 15W | F

> Ah! Energy-saving <u>bulbs</u> ... that makes a bit more sense. Now, I wonder if they've got any solar-powered apples?

Clever clues

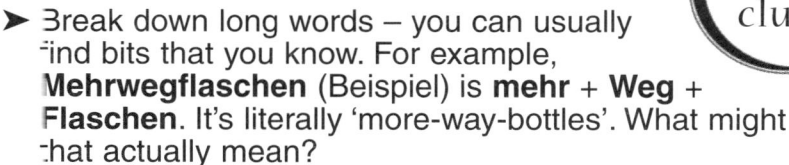

➤ Break down long words – you can usually find bits that you know. For example, **Mehrwegflaschen** (Beispiel) is **mehr** + **Weg** + **Flaschen**. It's literally 'more-way-bottles'. What might that actually mean?

➤ Some words are as easy as they look. **Saison** (text 2) is from French, but it looks very much like the English as well!

➤ **Birnen** (text 4) does mean 'pears' – but it means something else as well. A clue: they're the same shape.

Don't forget to check any hard words in the *Vital Vocabulary* (worksheet 72) if your memory needs a jog!

Name/
Group:

	PRO	KONTRA
Fahrrad	✔ Verbraucht keine Energie ✔ Keine Umweltverschmutzung (außer in der Fabrik!)	✘ Schlechtes Wetter! ✘ Kann keine Passagiere und kein Gepäck mitnehmen
Auto	✔ Verbraucht wenig Energie pro Person wenn voll ✔ „Grüne" Motoren kommen bald	✘ Oft nur mit einer Person besetzt ✘ Muss recycelt werden
Zug	✔ Kann „grüne" Energie verwenden ✔ Relativ sicher	✘ Nicht flexibel; kann nicht überall fahren ✘ Verbraucht viel Energie pro Person wenn leer
Bus	✔ Billig ✔ Sehr sparsam wenn voll	✘ Muss immer fahren – auch wenn leer ✘ Verwendet schmutzige Dieselmotoren
Flugzeug	✔ Das sicherste Transportmittel der Welt ✔ Sehr bequem und sehr schnell	✘ Viel Umweltverschmutzung, wo es am schlimmsten ist ✘ Kann keine „grüne" Energie verwenden

7 Read the analysis of the pros and cons of various types of transport. According to the text, which form of transport … (7 marks)

Beispiel: … can't use 'green' energy?   Plane

1 … has to be recycled?   _____

2 … can't carry passengers or luggage?   _____

3 … is the safest of all?   _____

4 … isn't flexible and can't go everywhere?   _____

5 … will soon have 'green' engines?   _____

6 … can use 'green' energy?   _____

7 … creates no pollution at all except during manufacture?   _____

This is what I call energy-saving transport!

☞ Handy hints

➤ **Kein**(e) comes up a lot here. Don't forget that, as a *negative*, it changes the meaning of the sentence completely!

➤ Lots of *modals* here, so look for main verbs at the ends of clauses.

➤ **Werden** (Auto text) is used to express the *passive*: to say what 'is being done' to something or someone. Here it's used with a modal – can you work out the meaning?

➤ Don't forget that, as well as meaning 'when' or 'whenever', **wenn** (Auto, Zug, Bus) has another meaning. What?

➤ **Voll** and **leer** (Auto, Bus) are useful opposites – what do they mean?

And finally, the *Vital Vocabulary* (worksheet 72) will help you with any of the specialized vocabulary you don't know.

Aludosen – Freund der Umwelt?
Lies weiter ...

Man findet Aludosen als Müll überall in Deutschland. Die Zahl der Dosen nimmt dramatisch zu und man verbraucht jetzt pro Jahr ungefähr sechs Milliarden Aludosen in Deutschland – das sind fast 10% aller Getränkeverpackungen! Keine andere Verpackung ist so schlecht für die Umwelt wie die Aludose!

Aludosen verursachen Probleme bei der Herstellung und beim Recycling (und sie werden oft nicht recycelt). Im Vergleich zu Mehrwegflaschen verbrauchen Aludosen zweimal so viel Energie und verursachen viermal so viele Treibhausgase, mehr FCKWs (die sehr schlecht für die Ozonschicht sind), mehr Verkehrslärm und mehr Müll.

Was können Sie als Kunde/Kundin tun? Sie können Flaschen aus Glas oder Kunststoff kaufen! Wenn man keine Dosen kauft, werden die Hersteller sich schnell umstellen müssen.

1 Beantworte die Fragen.

Beispiel: Wo findet man heutzutage Aludosen?

   Überall in Deutschland   (1 mark)

1 Wie viele Aludosen verbraucht man pro Jahr in Deutschland?

                                (1 mark)

2 Wann verursachen Aludosen Probleme?

                                (2 marks)

3 Wie viel Energie verbrauchen Aludosen im Vergleich zu Mehrwegflaschen?

                                (1 mark)

4 Warum sind FCKWs ein besonderes Problem?

                                (1 mark)

5 Was können die Kunden tun?

                                (1 mark)

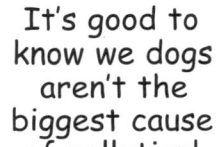

It's good to know we dogs aren't the biggest cause of pollution!

👉 Handy hints

➤ Try to pick out the **key words**. You may not have come across the separable verb **zunehmen (nimmt zu)**, but the meaning should be guessable from the context and from **sechs Milliarden**.

➤ Get those key words broken down! **Getränkedosen** and **Getränkepackungen** look dauntingly long – until you look closely at them!

➤ You probably know **Umwelt** because it's such a key word. If you don't, it literally means 'world around (us)'.

➤ Look for **set phrases** with **dative** prepositions, like **bei der** or **beim**, **zum** or **zur**, and work out their meaning from the context. The prepositions in these phrases often don't have their usual meanings, but convey things like 'in being …' or 'while being …' or 'in the … process'.

➤ We don't have many **Mehrwegflaschen** (Qu 3) here – Germany is way ahead of us in environmental matters – but you should be able to guess the word's meaning from knowing **Flasche** and **Weg**.

Check long compound words and very difficult words in the *Vital Vocabulary* (worksheet 73), as usual.

Pro und *kontra*: *Flugreisen* ✈

Ist es zu gefährlich geworden, mit dem Flugzeug zu reisen? Oder gehören Flugreisen einfach zum Leben im 21. Jahrhundert mit dazu? Wir haben mit Claudia, Julius und Karel aus Berlin gesprochen um herauszufinden, was sie über dieses Thema denken.

✔ *Pro*   **Claudia**, 16

Ich finde, dass man sich unser heutiges Leben ohne Flugreisen einfach nicht mehr vorstellen kann. Im Urlaub wollen die Leute doch gern exotische Reiseziele so schnell wie möglich erreichen. Da ist das Flugzeug doch die beste Variante. Ich möchte ja in den Ferien auch lieber nach Spanien, Australien oder Ägypten fahren als in Deutschland bleiben. Das ist mir einfach nicht aufregend genug.

? *Vielleicht*   **Julius**, 18

Viele Leute müssen beruflich reisen und ohne Flugzeuge würden sie für ihre Dienstreisen wahrscheinlich Tage oder Wochen brauchen.

Aber manchmal muss man zu irgendwelchen Meetings nach z.B. Amerika oder England, und so weit zu fliegen, um an einem einstündigen Meeting teilzunehmen, das geht nicht! Meiner Meinung nach könnte man viele Entscheidungen, die in Meetings getroffen werden von Businessleuten, die rund um die Welt fliegen, auch in Telefon-Konferenzen treffen.

✘ *Kontra*   **Karel**, 17

Aus meiner Sicht gibt es zwei Gründe, die gegen Flugreisen sprechen: die Umweltverschmutzung und das Sicherheitsrisiko. Wenn man sich überlegt, wie viel Kerosin verbraucht und wie viele Abgase in die Luft gepumpt werden, nur damit ein paar Leute ein langes Wochenende in New York verbringen und günstig einkaufen können, dann scheint mir das eine absolute Verschwendung zu sein. Ich bin völlig gegen Vielfliegerei. Das ist weder für die Umwelt noch für die Menschen gut.

VIELFLIEGER

1 Wer meint das? (5 marks)

Beispiel: Flugzeuge verbrauchen viel Treibstoff und verschmutzen die Luft.
                                            Karel

1 Man könnte Meetings rund um die Welt vermeiden.   _____

2 Man sollte zu einem kurzen Meeting nicht nach England fliegen.   _____

3 Vielfliegerei ist nicht gut für die Umwelt.   _____

4 Es ist schwer, sich ein Leben ohne Flugzeuge vorzustellen.   _____

5 Die meisten Deutschen möchten lieber im Ausland als in Deutschland Urlaub machen.   _____

> **Tips for texts**

> ➤ In true/false/can't tell, multiple-choice or 'who said it' questions you can often give yourself a good chance of a right answer, even if you're not sure, by *eliminating* any answers you're certain are wrong and then guessing among the remaining options.

> ➤ Always look carefully at the *questions*, because they usually give the same information as in the text, but often phrased more simply! For instance, **wie viele Abgase in die Luft gepumpt werden** and **Flugzeuge ... verschmutzen die Luft** are two ways of expressing the same thing.

> ➤ After verbs like **finden**, **denken** and **sagen**, you will often find the word **dass**. This is important because it sends the verb in the following clause to the end – and it's this verb that may well unlock the meaning.

> ➤ Lots of *modals* here – they also send the verb to the end of the clause, and this may conceal the meaning until you find it!

> ➤ **Weder ... noch** is a useful phrase to know, and a disastrous one not to know. It's a *concealed negative*, so be careful!

> ➤ Learn to *ignore* words that are really just sentence-fillers, used to pad out speech and emphasize points. What examples can you find in this text?

> ➤ Do you know what **um ... zu** means? It's a very useful and frequently used construction that introduces the *reason* for doing something.

Name/
Group:

A **B** **C** **D**

E **F** **G** **H** **I**

1 *Meine Familie:* Schreib den richtigen Buchstaben in jedes Kästchen. (5 marks)

Beispiel: *Meine Mutter ist Ärztin.* **C**

1 *Meine jüngere Schwester ist Angestellte.* ☐

2 *Mein Vater ist Briefträger.* ☐

3 *Mein Onkel ist Fußballspieler.* ☐

4 *Meine Tante ist Tischlerin.* ☐

5 *Meine ältere Schwester ist Stewardess.* ☐

Clever clues

➤ You can give yourself a little help by working out which jobs go with the pictures of **women**. Usually, in German, you simply add **-in** to the end of a word to make it feminine, but **Angestellte(r)** (text 1) is different: with an **-e** on the end it can be masculine or feminine (**der/die Angestellte**), and with an **-r** on the end it's masculine (**ein Angestellter**).

➤ Do you know your jobs?

• First eliminate the obvious ones, like **Fußballspieler** (text 3) and **Stewardess** (text 5) …

• For the others, break down words as usual. You should know **Brief** (text 2); what job can you think of that involves working with letters, postcards, etc.? And if you know **Tisch**, you should be able to work out what a **Tischler(in)** (text 4) does for a living!

There aren't many difficult new words here, but the *Vital Vocabulary* (worksheet 72) is there if you need it.

Name/
Group:

1 Wähl einen Job für jede Person. (5 marks)

A	Kfz-Mechaniker
B	Journalistin
C	Lehrer
D	Krankenpfleger
E	Pilot
F	Programmiererin
G	Bauer
H	Friseur

Beispiel: Ich möchte eine Karriere in den Medien. **B**

1 Ich möchte gern mit Kindern arbeiten. ☐

2 Die Computerindustrie interessiert mich sehr. ☐

3 Ich möchte viel reisen. ☐

4 Ich möchte in der Autoindustrie arbeiten. ☐

5 Ich interessiere mich sehr für Landwirtschaft. ☐

Ich möchte in der Wurstindustrie arbeiten!!

Clever clues

➤ How many **modal verbs** can you find in this text? Remember that they send the verb they're used with to the end of the sentence.

➤ There are several **compound nouns** here (i.e. nouns made up of two or more others), but some have **-industrie** in, which is similar to the English.

Again there isn't too much new vocabulary here, but the *Vital Vocabulary* (worksheet 72) is there as a last resort!

Name/
Group:

Ich würde nie Drogen probieren. Drogen sind ein Todesurteil.
Maria, 18

Rauchen außer Haus ist selbstsüchtig. Ich würde nur zu Hause rauchen.
Kai, 16

Ich würde rauchen, aber nur ein bisschen, weil Zigaretten sehr teuer sind.
Ali, 19

Im Prinzip bin ich nicht gegen das Rauchen, aber ich habe Angst vor Lungenkrebs.
Niklas, 20

Ich bin nicht grundsätzlich gegen Drogen, aber sie geben den Händlern zu viel Macht.
Sophie, 17

Haschisch ist nur ein Problem, weil es illegal ist. Ich würde es legalisieren.
Anita, 18

I don't smoke and I don't drink. But guess what I'm addicted to!

1 Lies die „Vox pops" und beantworte die Fragen. (5 marks)
Wer …

Beispiel:

… ist prinzipiell gegen Drogen?

Maria

1 … würde Haschisch legal machen?
_____

2 … würde nicht im Freien rauchen?
_____

3 … findet Rauchen zu teuer?
_____

4 … hat Angst, dass er krank wird?
_____

5 … denkt an die Drogenhändler?
_____

👉 Handy hints

➤ Look for key words: **Drogen**, **Rauchen**, **Lungenkrebs**, etc.

➤ Don't forget that *modals* and words like **weil** send the main verb to the end of the clause, and this is crucial because the verb often unlocks the meaning of the sentence.

➤ **Angst haben vor** (Niklas) is a funny phrase. Literally it means 'to have fear in front of' – what would we say?

➤ Look for *paraphrasing* again: clues you can find in the questions, which say what is in the text in a different way, e.g. **im Freien** (Qu 2)/**außer Haus** (Kai) **rauchen**.

If there's still a word you don't know, have a look in the *Vital Vocabulary* (worksheet 72).

Name/
Group:

Studium ... ... **oder Lehre?**

Speech bubble: *Studium oder Schläfchen? Kommt nicht in Frage – wenn ich studiere, schlafe ich ein!*

AKTUELL: Was wollt ihr machen, wenn ihr mit der Schule fertig seid? Findet ihr ein Studium oder eine Berufsausbildung besser?

Anna: Für mich auf keinen Fall ein Studium. Dreizehn Jahre Schule sind für mich wirklich genug. Ich mache lieber eine Berufsausbildung.

Mirto: Ich werde wahrscheinlich etwas Technisches studieren.

David: Ich höre gut zu und kann persönliche Probleme analysieren. Deshalb möchte ich später Psychologie studieren.

AKTUELL: Welche Vorteile seht ihr bei eurer Entscheidung?

Mirto: Ich finde ein Studium gut, weil man danach verschiedene Sachen machen kann. Wenn man eine Ausbildung macht, kann man danach nur auf einem bestimmten Gebiet arbeiten. Nach einem Studium gibt es verschiedene Perspektiven.

Anna: Ich finde eine Berufsausbildung besser als ein Studium, weil sie viel praxisorientierter ist. Außerdem dauert eine Berufsausbildung nur drei Jahre, man kann also früher sein eigenes Geld verdienen.

David: Für mich kommt eigentlich nur ein Studium in Frage, weil man anders nicht Psychologe werden kann. Der Vorteil beim Studium ist, dass man sich lange mit interessanten Themen beschäftigen kann. ■

---

1 Füll die Lücken mit dem passenden Namen aus. (5 marks)

Beispiel: ___Anna___ hat nicht vor, ein Studium zu machen.

1 _____ hat die Absicht ein technisches Fach zu studieren.

2 _____ hört seinen Freunden gut zu und kann ihnen oft bei ihren Problemen helfen.

3 _____ möchte an Themen arbeiten, die er wirklich interessant findet.

4 _____ findet eine Berufsausbildung besser, weil man früher unabhängig ist.

5 _____ möchte keine Ausbildung machen, weil ihn das einschränken könnte.

Tips for texts

➤ Don't miss **concealed negatives** which reverse the meaning of the sentence. They are important and tricky – and disastrous if you miss them! **Auf keinen Fall** (Anna) is one: what does it mean?

➤ Lots of **compound words** here – don't be put off by their length. They are often just composed of easy words that you already know, but sometimes the joins are hard to find. Look for a word within a word that you recognize and break the compound word where the word you recognize begins or ends.

➤ **Bei** (Aktuell) has a lot of meanings, depending on its context. As here, it often means 'in' or 'concerning'.

Name/
Group:

Vital Vocabulary

The environment

◆ Foundation and ◆ ◆ Foundation/Higher (WS 64–65)

Nouns

Feminine
die Energiesparbirne	energy-saving light bulb
die Fabrik	factory
die Mehrwegflasche	returnable bottle
die Umweltver- schmutzung	environmental pollution

Neuter
das Altpapier	used paper
das Baden	having a bath
das Duschen	having a shower
das Gepäck	luggage
das Transportmittel	means of transport

One way to remember long lists of words is to write each one in a different style, colour or typeface. This way, every word will have a character of its own, which will help you fix it in your mind.

Verbs and useful expressions

außer	except
bald	soon
benutzen	to use
bequem	comfortable
besetzt	occupied
billig	cheap
drin	in it
lassen	to leave
leer	empty
recyceln	to recycle
am schlimmsten	worst
schmutzig	dirty
sicher	safe, sure
sparen	to save
sparsam	economical
überall	everywhere
verbrauchen	to use, consume
verwenden	to use
voll	full

Careers, future and social issues

◆ Foundation and ◆ ◆ Foundation/Higher (WS 68–70)

Nouns

Masculine
der/die Angestellte	office worker
der Arzt/die Ärztin	doctor
der Briefträger/ die Briefträgerin	postman/woman
der Friseur/ die Friseurin	hairdresser
der Fußballspieler/ die Fußballspielerin	football player
der Händler	dealer
der Lungenkrebs	lung cancer
der Tischler/ die Tischlerin	carpenter

Feminine
die Angst	fear, worry
die (Auto)industrie	(car) industry
die Droge	drug
die Karriere	career
die Landwirtschaft	agriculture
die Macht	power
die Stewardess	stewardess
die Zigarette	cigarette

Neuter
das Haschisch	cannabis
das Kind	child
das Rauchen	smoking
das Todesurteil	death sentence

Plural
die Medien	the media

Verbs and useful expressions

außer Haus	outside
ein bisschen	a bit
im Freien	in the open air
grundsätzlich	basically
sich interessieren für	to be interested in
legalisieren	to legalize
prinzipiell	in principle
probieren	to try
selbstsüchtig	selfish
teuer	dear, expensive
ich würde	I would

When you're near the end of your course, it's a good idea to go through the Vital Vocabulary and note down any words you still don't know. Then you'll have a shorter and more manageable list – and keep doing it, so that the list gets shorter and shorter!

Name/
Group:

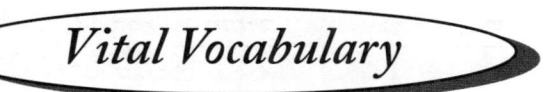

Vital Vocabulary

The environment
◆ ◆ ◆ Higher (WS 66–67)

Nouns

Masculine

der Grund	*reason*
der Kunde/die Kundin	*customer*
der Kunststoff	*plastic*
der Müll	*rubbish*
der Treibstoff	*fuel*

Feminine

die Aludose	*aluminium can*
die Dienstreise	*business journey*
die Flugreise	*flight, flying*
die Herstellung	*manufacture*
die Mehrwegflasche	*returnable bottle*
die Milliarde	*billion (1,000 million)*
die Ozonschicht	*ozone layer*
die Umweltverschmutzung	*environmental pollution*
die Variante	*alternative, variant*
die Verpackung	*packaging*
die Verschwendung	*waste*
die Vielfliegerei	*frequent flying*

Neuter

das Reiseziel	*destination*
das Sicherheitsrisiko	*safety risk*
das Treibhausgas	*greenhouse gas*

Plural

die Abgase	*exhaust gases*
die FCKWs	*CFCs*

Verbs and useful expressions

aufregend	*exciting*
beruflich	*on business, professional(ly)*
einstündig	*one-hour (long)*
eine Entscheidung treffen	*to come to a decision*
günstig	*cheap*
heutig	*today's*
irgendwelche(r/s)	*some or other*
so schnell wie möglich	*as quickly as possible*
aus meiner Sicht	*from my point of view*
teilnehmen	*to take part*
sich (dat.) überlegen	*to consider*
sich umstellen	*to switch over*
verbrauchen	*to use, consume*
vermeiden	*to avoid*
verschmutzen	*to pollute*
verursachen	*to create, produce*
sich (dat.) vorstellen	*to imagine*
weder … noch	*neither … nor*
zunehmen	*to increase*

A good vocabulary practice exercise is to write some words on small cards and then cover each one up. Then gradually remove the covers – how little of the word can you uncover before you 'get' it? Try to improve on your best efforts!

One way of making vocabulary learning less painful is to put a little time aside every day for doing absolutely nothing else. But make it pleasant: relax, maybe put some music on, get a drink or something to eat, and just concentrate on the words for, say, 20 minutes.

Careers, future and social issues
◆ ◆ ◆ Higher (WS 71)

Nouns

Masculine

der Psychologe/ die Psychologin	*psychologist*
der Vorteil	*advantage*

Feminine

die Berufsausbildung	*vocational training*
die Entscheidung	*decision*
die Lehre	*apprenticeship*

Neuter

das Gebiet	*area*
das Studium	*study*

Verbs and useful expressions

analysieren	*to analyse*
angenehm	*pleasant*
ins Ausland	*(to) abroad*
außerdem	*besides*
sich beschäftigen mit	*to concern/occupy oneself with*
einschränken	*to restrict*
auf keinen Fall	*under no circumstances*
fertig	*ready, finished*
praxisorientiert	*vocationally orientated*
unabhängig	*independent*
verschieden	*different*
zuhören	*to listen (to)*

Name/ Group:	© Mary Glasgow Magazines 2003	73

Section A
Questions and answers in English

▼ Read these signs giving environmental advice and answer the questions.

Stellen Sie Ihren Motor bitte ab!

1 What does this sign tell you to do in a traffic jam? (1 mark)

_____

Abfall immer in die Mülltonne oder zum Recyclingcontainer bringen!

2 Which TWO places could you take your rubbish to? (2 marks)

_____

Benutzen Sie keine Spraydosen!

3 What shouldn't you use? (1 mark)

_____

Section B
Fragen und Antworten auf Deutsch

▼ Lies die Sätze über die Zukunft. Wer möchte was machen? Wähl den richtigen Buchstaben.
(5 marks)

Beispiel: Wenn ich mit der Schule fertig bin, möchte ich Lastwagenfahrerin werden.
Lora `B`

1 Ich gehe nicht gern zur Schule und deshalb suche ich einen Job in einem Supermarkt.
Katrin ☐

2 Meine Mutter war Ärztin und dieser Job interessiert mich auch.
Lars ☐

3 Ich interessiere mich für Oldtimer-Autos und möchte gern Kfz-Mechaniker werden.
Lutz ☐

4 Ich kann gut singen und Gitarre spielen und habe die Absicht in einer Band zu spielen.
Gisela ☐

5 Ich hoffe auf der Uni zu studieren und möglicherweise Psychologe zu werden.
Klaus ☐

Name/
Group:

1

Was findet ihr an anderen **schön** oder **attraktiv**?

Diese Frage haben wir zwei Jugendlichen gestellt.

Nele: Ich finde es attraktiv, wenn jemand irgendwie interessant ist. Also, wie soll ich das sagen, wenn sich jemand nicht nur für sein Aussehen interessiert, sondern auch viele Dinge macht und Hobbys hat. Sicher gefallen mir Jungs, die gut gestylt sind und eine sportliche Figur haben. Aber wenn man sich dann mit denen nicht gut unterhalten kann, weil sie sich für nichts interessieren, dann finde ich das ziemlich langweilig. Ich suche mir meine Freundinnen ja auch nicht danach aus, wie sie aussehen, sondern danach, was ich mit denen unternehmen kann und ob ich mit ihnen Spaß haben kann.

Carina: Ich sehe das so ähnlich. Ich finde Leute gut, die Humor haben und nicht alles immer gleich negativ sehen. Denn das geht mir völlig auf die Nerven. In meiner alten Clique war das immer so. Wir haben den ganzen Nachmittag herumgehangen und immer nur darüber geredet, wie ungerecht und schlecht alles ist. Aber wir haben nie etwas getan um irgendeine Situation zu verbessern. Es hat eine Weile gedauert, bis ich begriffen habe, was da abläuft. Jetzt treffe ich mich kaum noch mit den Leuten aus meiner Clique und mache mehr mit meiner neuen Freundin. Jana sieht alles positiver als ich. Durch sie habe ich gelernt, nicht immer nur zu meckern, sondern einfach etwas zu tun. Und wenn ich neue Leute kennen lerne, ist es mir jetzt viel wichtiger als früher, dass sie positiv drauf sind.

1 Lies den Text 1. Schreib **R** (richtig), **F** (falsch) oder **?** (nicht im Text). (5 marks)

Beispiel:

Nele interessiert sich für hässliche Jungs. [F]

1 Nele findet interessante Leute am attraktivsten. ☐

2 Nele sucht sich nur Freundinnen aus, die gut aussehen. ☐

3 Carina findet Leute, die oft lachen, attraktiv. ☐

4 Carinas alte Clique war etwas deprimierend für sie. ☐

5 Carina hat jetzt Freundinnen, die negativ drauf sind. ☐

2

Ein sparsames Auto

Das Team der Loremo Automotive GmbH arbeitet gerade an einem super-sparsamen Auto, das weniger Benzin verbrauchen soll als alle bisherigen Spar-Modelle. Das neue Spar-Auto heißt kurz L22 und verbraucht nur 1,5 Liter auf 100 Kilometer. Es wiegt weniger als 450 Kilogramm und erreicht Höchstgeschwindigkeiten von bis zu 140 Kilometer pro Stunde. Vom Design her sieht das 1,5 Liter Auto wie ein kleiner Sportflitzer aus und es ist nicht erst dann umweltfreundlich, wenn es auf der Straße fährt. Schon bei der Herstellung verbraucht der L22 nur etwa ein Drittel der Energie, die für die Produktion herkömmlicher PKWs benötigt wird. Der L22 wird aus recycelbaren Materialien hergestellt und die Produktion des sparsamen Flitzers erzeugt nur ein Drittel des Abfalls, der bei einem normalen Auto produziert wird. Das bedeutet pro Auto etwa 15 Tonnen Abfall weniger.

2 Lies den Text 2 und beantworte die Fragen auf Deutsch. (5 marks)

Beispiel: Was ist der Loremo L22?   *Ein super-sparsames Auto*

1 Welche Höchstgeschwindigkeit kann der L22 erreichen? _____

2 Wie viel Benzin verbraucht der L22? _____

3 Wie sieht das Auto aus? _____

4 Aus welchen Materialien wird der L22 gebaut? _____

5 Wie viel Abfall produziert man bei der Herstellung eines L22s, im Vergleich zu einem normalen Auto? _____

Name/ Group:

8 Personal details: Foundation (1)

1 1 C, 2 D, 3 E, 4 A, 5 B   (5 marks)

9 Personal details: Foundation (2)

1 1 Johannes, 2 Monika, 3 Otto, 4 Monika,
5 Johannes   (5 marks)

10 Personal details: Foundation/Higher

1 1 F, 2 F, 3 F, 4 R, 5 ?, 6 F   (6 marks)
2 1 D, 2 A, 3 B, 4 C, 5 H   (5 marks)

11 Personal details: Higher

1 1 a Three: Got a ballet skirt and danced
       around the flat, b Five: Began ballet
       lessons, c Ten: Started training properly
                                      (3 marks)
   2 Ballet videos, ballet books, ballet
       clothes for Christmas and birthday
                                      (3 marks)
   3 Three of: Join a dance class, Study at
       the Hamburg State Opera or in
       Wuppertal, Dance on all the great
       stages of the world, Be fêted as a
       prima ballerina   (3 marks)
2 1 Ballett-Videos, Ballett-Bücher und
       Ballett-Klamotten
   2 Fünf Jahre alt
   3 Zehn Jahre alt
   4 Jeden Nachmittag
   5 An der Hamburger Staatsoper oder
       in Wuppertal   (5 marks)

12 Interests and hobbies: Foundation

1 [A], C, E, F   (3 marks)

13 Interests and hobbies: Foundation/Higher (1)

1 Mittag: Ankunftsparty in der Aula D
Vierzehn Uhr: Tischtennis für alle! F
Schwimmparty am Freibad! Pünktlich um
sechzehn Uhr C
Ab 20 Uhr: Disko. Bring einen Freund/
eine Freundin mit! B   (4 marks)

14 Interests and hobbies: Foundation/Higher (2)

1 1 B, 2 E, 3 H, 4 G, 5 F   (5 marks)

15 Interests and hobbies: Higher

1 1 R, 2 R, 3 F, 4 F   (4 marks)
2 1 Wenn das Meer zu ruhig zum
       Surfen war   (1 mark)
   2 Bessere Räder   (1 mark)
   3 Aluminium, Plastik und Fiberglas
                                      (3 marks)
   4 Die Kids in den Großstädten   (1 mark)

18 Home and local environment: Foundation (1)

1 1 C, D   (2 marks)
   2 A, D   (2 marks)
   3 A, C, D   (3 marks)

19 Home and local environment: Foundation (2)

1 H, C, E, A, F   (5 marks)

20 Home and local environment: Foundation/Higher

1 1 F, 2 ?, 3 F, 4 R, 5 F   (5 marks)

21 Home and local environment: Higher

1 (Alternative phrasing acceptable if
language and facts correct)
   1 Ziemlich ruhig
   2 Rasen, Bäume und Blumenbeete
   3 Zehn Minuten
   4 Weil es in der Stadtmitte eine Klinik,
       eine Post (usw.) gibt
   5 Im vierten Stock
   6 Weil der Aufzug oft außer Betrieb ist
   7 Damit er (eines Tages) eine Katze
       haben kann   (7 marks)

22 Test yourself 1: Foundation & Foundation/Higher

A 1 Smoke; Walk on the grass   (2 marks)
   2 The old town; Pedestrians   (2 marks)
B 1 H, 2 A, 3 G, 4 B, 5 C   (5 marks)

23 Test yourself 1: Higher

1 1 R, 2 F, 3 R, 4 ?, 5 F   (5 marks)
2 1 Johannes, 2 Zoltan, 3 Johannes,
   4 Zoltan, 5 Zoltan   (5 marks)

24 Transport and finding the way: Foundation (1)

1 1 In an emergency (1 mark)
2 Next to the ticket window (1 mark)
3 1–3: Local trains
4–7: Express trains
8–10: Intercity and international trains (3 marks)

25 Transport and finding the way: Foundation (2)

1 A 300 m, B 0,5 km, C 2 km, D 1 km,
E 100 m, F 200 m (5 marks)

26 Transport and finding the way: Foundation/Higher

1 1 Halle, 2 Bahnhof, 3 Mittag, 4 24 Euro,
5 Geld, 6 Bus (6 marks)

27 Transport and finding the way: Higher

1 1 Urlaub, 2 Cyber-Reisen, 3 nichts,
4 Umwelt (4 marks)
2 1 C, 2 C, 3 B, 4 A (4 marks)

30 Tourism and accommodation: Foundation (1)

1 1 A, 2 C, 3 B, 4 C, 5 D (5 marks)

31 Tourism and accommodation: Foundation (2)

1 1 B, 2 E, 3 D, 4 H, 5 C (5 marks)

32 Tourism and accommodation: Foundation/Higher

1 1 R, 2 F, 3 ?, 4 F, 5 R (5 marks)

33 Tourism and accommodation: Higher

1 1 Anke, 2 Anke, 3 Kirsten, 4 Kirsten,
5 Anke (5 marks)
2 1 C, 2 D, 3 B (3 marks)

34 Holiday activities and services: Foundation (1)

1 1 (Cheese on) toast and (green)
salad (2 marks)
2 Chicken (1 mark)
3 One (1 mark)
4 A pot (1 mark)
5 Yes (1 mark)

35 Holiday activities and services: Foundation (2)

1 [A Berlin], B Dresden, C Hamburg,
D München, E Frankfurt (4 marks)

36 Holiday activities and services: Foundation/Higher

1 1 Anja, 2 Judith, 3 Melanie, 4 Melanie,
5 Judith (5 marks)

37 Holiday activities and services: Higher

1 (Alternative phrasing acceptable if
language and facts correct)
1 Das DB-Museum/Eisenbahnmuseum
2 Im Herzen der Altstadt
3 Klein und dünn
4 Zu Weihnachten/In der
Weihnachtszeit (4 marks)
2 1 C, 2 B, 3 B, 4 C (4 marks)

40 Test yourself 2: Foundation & Foundation/Higher

1 1 G, 2 E, 3 F, 4 D, 5 A (5 marks)
2 1 R, 2 F, 3 R, 4 F, 5 F (5 marks)

41 Test yourself 2: Higher

1 1 A, 2 C, 3 D, 4 C (4 marks)
2 1 Germany and England (2 marks)
2 A publishing house (1 mark)
3 Because they were on towns listed
in the Baedeker guides (1 mark)
4 City tours (1 mark)
5 1855 (1 mark)

42 Home, health and fitness: Foundation (1)

1 1 E, 2 B, 3 A, 4 G, 5 F (5 marks)
2 1 E, 2 C, 3 B, 4 D, 5 A (5 marks)

43 Home, health and fitness: Foundation (2)

1 1 F, **2** D, **3** I, **4** E, **5** B (5 marks)

2 Hauptspeise: [Brot], Salami, Käse
  (2 marks)

  Nachtisch: Jogurt, Obst (2 marks)
  Getränk: Milch (1 mark)

44 Home, health and fitness: Foundation/Higher

1 1 R, **2** ?, **3** R, **4** F, **5** R (5 marks)

45 Home, health and fitness: Higher

1 1 Janina, **2** Michaela, **3** Margrit, **4** Margrit, **5** Wiebke (5 marks)

46 Work and shopping: Foundation (1)

1 1 Bean soup, **2** Crisps, **3** 1.50 euros a bar, **4** Yoghurt (4 marks)

2 1 F, **2** C, **3** B, **4** A (4 marks)

47 Work and shopping: Foundation (2)

1 1 D, **2** F, **3** B, **4** G, **5** A (5 marks)

2 [A 2], **B** 1, **C** U, **D** E, **E** 3, **F** 2 (5 marks)

48 Work and shopping: Foundation/Higher

1 1 E, **2** A, **3** C, **4** B, **5** E (5 marks)

49 Work and shopping: Higher

1 1 Jella, **2** Carla, **3** Carla, **4** Arno, **5** Carla (5 marks)

52 Leisure: Foundation (1)

1 1 ✗, **2** ✔, **3** ✔, **4** ✗, **5** ✗ (5 marks)

53 Leisure: Foundation (2)

1 1 Lena, **2** Katharina, **3** Laura, **4** Lukas, **5** Tobias (5 marks)

54 Leisure: Foundation/Higher

1 1 F, **2** ?, **3** F, **4** R, **5** F (5 marks)

55 Leisure: Higher

1 1 Holland
2 Getting from place to place quickly (in winter)
3 1784
4 The 'Wiener Eislaufverein' in Austria
5 Men
6 1906
7 The (ice-skating) World Championships (7 marks)

56 Test yourself 3: Foundation & Foundation/Higher

1

GESUND	UNGESUND	
[apples]	[cakes]	
grapes	chocolate	(2 marks)
eggs	chips	(2 marks)
salad	sweets	(2 marks)
pasta	crisps	(2 marks)
chicken	hamburgers	(2 marks)

2 1 Gardening
2 Delivering newspapers
3 Working in a supermarket
4 Washing cars
5 Waiter/Waitress (5 marks)

57 Test yourself 3: Higher

1 1 Erika, **2** Birgit, **3** Erika, **4** Birgit, **5** Erika (5 marks)

2 1 F, **2** R, **3** F, **4** R, **5** ? (5 marks)

58 Character and relationships: Foundation (1)

1 1 Herr Schröder, **2** Tricksi (Silke's dog), **3** Anke, **4** Otto, **5** Silke's mother (5 marks)

59 Character and relationships: Foundation (2)

1 1 R, **2** F, **3** ?, **4** R, **5** F (5 marks)

2 1 Jonas, **2** Jonas, **3** Sophie, **4** Alexander, **5** Laura (5 marks)

60 Character and relationships: Foundation/Higher

1 1 Gabi, **2** Wiebke, **3** Jörg, **4** Wiebke, **5** Lutz (5 marks)

61 Character and relationships: Higher

1 1 B, 2 C, 3 D, 4 A   (4 marks)

2 1 F, 2 R, 3 ?, 4 R   (4 marks)

64 The environment: Foundation

1 1 F, 2 C, 3 A, 4 E, 5 D   (5 marks)

65 The environment: Foundation/Higher

1 1 car, 2 bicycle, 3 plane, 4 train, 5 car, 6 train, 7 bicycle   (7 marks)

66 The environment: Higher (1)

1 (Alternative phrasing acceptable if language and facts correct)
1 Sechs Milliarden   (1 mark)
2 Bei der Herstellung und beim Recycling   (2 marks)
3 Zweimal so viel   (1 mark)
4 Weil sie schlecht für die Ozonschicht sind   (1 mark)
5 Sie können Flaschen aus Glas oder Kunststoff kaufen.   (1 mark)

67 The environment: Higher (2)

1 1 Julius, 2 Julius, 3 Karel, 4 Claudia, 5 Claudia   (5 marks)

68 Careers, future and social issues: Foundation (1)

1 1 B, 2 G, 3 A, 4 H, 5 E   (5 marks)

69 Careers, future and social issues: Foundation (2)

1 1 C, 2 F, 3 E, 4 A, 5 G   (5 marks)

70 Careers, future and social issues: Foundation/Higher

1 1 Anita, 2 Kai, 3 Ali, 4 Niklas, 5 Sophie   (5 marks)

71 Careers, future and social issues: Higher

1 1 Mirto, 2 David, 3 David, 4 Anna, 5 Mirto   (5 marks)

74 Test yourself 4: Foundation & Foundation/Higher

A 1 Switch your engine off   (1 mark)
2 Rubbish bin/skip or recycling container   (2 marks)
3 Spray cans/Aerosols   (1 mark)

B 1 I, 2 H, 3 G, 4 C, 5 A   (5 marks)

75 Test yourself 4: Higher

1 1 R, 2 F, 3 R, 4 R, 5 F   (5 marks)

2 1 140 km/h
2 1,5 Liter auf 100 Kilometer
3 Wie ein kleiner Sportflitzer
4 Aus recycelbaren Materialien
5 15 Tonnen weniger   (5 marks)